R. D. Bartlett and Patricia P. Bartlett

Geckos

Everything about Selection, Care, Nutrition,
Diseases, Breeding, and Behavior

With 60 Color Photographs by R. D. Bartlett

Illustrations by Tom Kerr

BARRON'S

All inquiries should be addressed to:
Barron's Educational Series, Inc.
250 Wireless Boulevard
Hauppauge, New York 11788

International Standard Book No. 0-8120-9082-9

Library of Congress Catalog Card No. 95-3640

Library of Congress Cataloging-in-Publication Data
Bartlett, Richard D., 1938–
    Geckos : everything about selection, care, nutrition, diseases, breeding, and behavior / R. D. Bartlett and Patricia P. Bartlett ; with color photographs by R. D. Bartlett.
       p.   cm.
    Includes index.
    ISBN 0–8120–9082–9
    1. Geckos as pets. 2. Geckos. I. Bartlett, Patricia Pope, 1949– . II. Title.
SF459.G35B37 1995
639.3′95—dc20   95–3640
                          CIP

Printed in Hong Kong

6789   9955   9

About the Authors

R. D. Bartlett is a herpetologist who has authored more than 350 articles and three books on reptiles. He lectures extensively and has participated in field studies across North and Latin America.

In 1978 he began the Reptilian Breeding and Research Institute (RBRI), a private facility. Since its inception, more than 150 species of reptiles and amphibians have been bred at RBRI, some for the first time in the United States under captive conditions. Successes at the RBRI include several endangered species.

Bartlett is a member of numerous herpetological and conservation organizations.

Patricia Bartlett received her B.S. from Colorado State University and became the editor for an outdoor book publisher in St. Petersburg, Florida. Subsequently, she worked for the science museum in Springfield, Massachusetts and for the historical museum in Ft. Myers, Florida. She is the author of five books on natural history and historical subjects.

Photos on the Covers

Front: *Phelsuma guimbeaui*
Inside front: *Naultinus elegans*
Inside back: *Hemidactylus tucicus*
Back: *Phelsuma seippi*

The illustration of the European leaf-toed gecko (page 66, top) is by Patricia Bartlett.

Important Notes

Before using any of the electrical equipment described in this book, be sure to read Avoiding Electrical Accidents on page 31.

While handling geckos you may occasionally receive bites or scratches. If your skin is broken, see your physician immediately.

Some terrarium plants may be harmful to the skin or mucous membranes of human beings. If you notice any signs of irritation, wash the area thoroughly. See your physician if the condition persists.

Geckos may transmit certain infections to humans. Always wash your hands carefully after handling your specimens. Always supervise children who wish to observe your geckos.

Contents

The beautiful Madagascar giant day gecko, Phelsuma madagascariensis grandis, *like most geckos, prefers a head-down stance.*

Preface

Geckos were a virtual unknown in the pet trade when I was growing up. Or at least they were an unknown until I discovered an ad by Quivira Specialties Co. in the back of an *Outdoor Life Magazine*. I replied to the ad and discovered the wonderful world of mail-order herpetology—and geckos.

I learned of the availability of tokay and day geckos and of Turkish and reef geckos. But money was tight back in those days, so, although I learned of the geckos, it was some time before I actually began meeting them. When I did meet them, it was not from Quivira.

I had met a middle school teacher, E. Gordon "Gordy" Johnston by name, who was also interested in reptiles and amphibians, and together we decided to place a small order with an Asian dealer. We did, and I soon got my first look at a tokay—a big, sullen gecko species attractively clad in hues of gray and orange. I quickly learned that the disposition of this species was as sullen as their lidless-eyed glower.

Following that first gecko encounter it seemed that geckos were every-where. I soon encountered day geckos, wonderfully clad in kelly green, at an animal importer's shop, Wild Cargo; Gordy received a few turnip-tailed geckos, 6 inches (15.2 cm) long and cryptically colored, from a friend in Central America, and one of his students visited the Virgin Islands and returned with some minuscule sphaerodactylines (I could hardly believe that such tiny lizards existed!).

A few years later I imported a few wildlife shipments from Pakistan. The supplier, Jerry Anderson, went out of his way to include some interesting geckos. I got to know turnip-tails, leopard (then uncommonly seen), and spider geckos on a firsthand basis.

Other shipments—from Kenya, Dahomey, South Africa, Australia, and other areas—allowed me to become familiar with additional geckos and convinced me that I would like to know these little lizards even better.

My chance for enhanced knowledge began somewhat later in life when I began making jaunts to Florida, Mexico, and countries in South America. In those places I saw geckos under debris in yards, catching roaches and other insects on the trunks of palms, and ghosting over motel walls and ceilings. Besides these natural encounters, I began breeding the lizards in captivity and have, over the years, succeeded in breeding thirty-five or forty species. Like those seen in the field, some have been common, others less so. All have been interesting.

Today (1994), a great many gecko species are bred by hobbyists and zookeepers. Leopard geckos, one of the hardiest, most handleable, and desirable species, are captive-bred by the thousands annually. Even such rarities as the New Caledonian giant geckos and New Zealand green geckos, once found only in the collections of the largest zoological gardens, are now in the hands of experienced private hobbyists. It is just possible that in the not too distant future these magnificent species will become more commonplace—but I doubt that they will ever become cheap.

In the pages that follow I have offered comments on some of the most basic aspects of gecko keeping as well as some on more advanced procedures. Intended as guidelines, these suggestions should be interpreted as just this: guidelines. They are methods that I have used successfully, but should by no means be construed as the only road to success. As you become more experienced, extrapolate and devise your own methods. There undoubtedly are many ways to streamline and enhance my suggestions.

By closely observing your animals and familiarizing yourself with their preferred habitats and their habits, you just might be the one to captive-breed a species for the first time.

How This Book is Organized: Throughout this book I have followed a narrative format in which I offer suggestions on caging, lighting, health, diet, and reproduction of geckos. I have also discussed the identification and husbandry of several dozen species, given some field lore, and even touched on photographic techniques. Among these species are all of the gecko species that may be encountered in the wild in North America, Northern Mexico, and Europe. I have also included a lengthy chapter about the beautiful and popular day geckos, comments on diverse leaf-tailed geckos, and an extensive discussion of the leopard and fat-tailed geckos.

I hope that you will find this approach both workable and informative.

Acknowledgments: Sincerest thanks to Bill Love and Rob McInnis of Glades Herp, Inc., and to Chris McQuade of Gulf Coast Reptiles for allowing me opportunities to photograph their geckos. Thanks also to Sean McKeown and the Chaffee Zoological Gardens for affording to me the opportunity to photograph several New Zealand and new Caledonian gecko species with which I was previously unfamiliar. To Tim Tytle, M.D., and Reid Taylor, M.D., my thanks for the many conversations, pointers, and exchanges of ideas. Certainly no one with a love for geckos could omit the contributions of Mike Miller, D.V.M., once a phelsumaphile in the truest sense. Thanks, also, to Rich Funk, D.V.M., for allowing use of the medication tables. Special thanks to our editor, Don Reis, for his patience and professionalism and to Fredric Frye, D.V.M., for critically reading and commenting on the manuscript.

What Is a Gecko?

Geckos are lizards most commonly found in subtropical and tropical regions. They share, to a greater or lesser degree, the following characteristics: no eyelids (the eyes are protected by a clear scale); retiring demeanor; nocturnal activity; and many have expanded toe-pads, which give these lizards the ability to climb walls, to cling to vertical rock faces, or to "hug" tree trunks or branches. Species coloration ranges from a quiet gray-brown to a bright kelly green.

Gecko Families

Geckos belong to the infraorder Gekkota, a grouping that, depending on the authority followed, includes either three or five lizard families.

The most liberal accounting delineates the families of the Gekkota as:

Eublepharidae: The eyelid geckos
Gekkonidae: The typical geckos
Dibamidae: The dibamid lizards
Xantusiidae: The night lizards
Pygopodidae: The Australian and New Guinean footless lizards.

The more conservative accounting of the infraorder Gekkota discounts the xantusids as members and continues to consider the eublepharine geckos as a subfamily, rather than as a full family.

Depending on whether you follow the conservative or liberal track, the gecko families can be divided as follows:

• Conservative
Family Gekkonidae
   Subfamily Eublepharinae
   Subfamily Gekkoninae
   Subfamily Sphaerodactylinae

• Liberal
Family Eublepharidae
Family Gekkonidae
   Subfamily Gekkoninae
   Subfamily Diplodactylinae
   Subfamily Sphaerodactylinae
(I opt for the more liberal viewpoint.)

The main difference between the two classification delineations relates to the eublepharines—the leopard, banded, and fat-tailed geckos. The eublepharines are the only geckos to have functional eyelids. Too, all eublepharines lack toe-pads and all lay soft-shelled eggs. Like many other geckos, eublepharines also have a voice.

The Subfamilies

In the family Gekkoninae:

Gekkonines lack eyelids and usually produce two hard-shelled eggs per clutch. They may or may not have toe-pads. These geckos can vocalize. Examples are the tokay and day geckos.

Diplodactylines lack eyelids but produce paired soft-shelled eggs. These species vocalize. Examples are the velvet and New Caledonian geckos as well as the Australian genus *Diplodactylus*. The toe-pads may vary from well developed to absent.

Sphaerodactylines lack eyelids and produce but a single egg per clutch. These are the tiny New World geckos; none can vocalize. Reef and ashy geckos are examples. Some species have prominent toe-pads; others lack them.

Where Are Geckos Found?

Geckos are well represented in the

What's in a Name?

Much is in a name, for it is by their names that we are able to identify and discuss the various animals and plants.

To systematists it is the "formal name," the name given at the time an organism is officially (scientifically) described, which is the most important. This is a standardized name, which is applicable only to a single species at a given time. As additional information is gathered, the original name given the organism might change, but these changes are made in a set and methodical manner. The changes and the reasons for them are published and any systematist who chooses can remain up to date and "in sync."

On the other hand, the other set of names—the common names—are often arbitrary. Let's use a bird for an example. The American robin, a thrush, was named because it reminded the English colonists of the European robin, a very different bird. Thus the same common name applies to two different birds. However, the scientific designations *Turdus migratorius* for the American bird and *Erithacus rubicola* for the European are different. Each applies to only the single species. There can

be no confusion about which species one is discussing when the scientific designation is used. This holds true for reptiles, and by extension, to geckos as well. To many folks, a gecko—any gecko—seen on a house is a "house gecko." And there are a lot of geckos, a lot of very different geckos, that are seen either regularly or infrequently on houses. However, if the term "house gecko" is mentioned to a herpetologist he or she will immediately ask "what kind?" If the answer was "*Hemidactylus turcicus*," there would be no confusion. Or how about a burrowing gecko? Do you know how many kinds of geckos there are that burrow? Well, there are a bunch. And if you were to ask me for information about a burrowing gecko, the best I could give you would be generalities. However, if you ask me for information about *Chondrodactylus angulifer*, I would immediately recognize the name (or be able to look it up) and would be in a position to supply you with the specifics you had wanted.

So, I urge you to begin learning and using scientific names. To do so will enable you to discuss your hobby with others, all of you secure in the knowledge that it is about the same species that you are speaking.

warmer climes of both the Old and New Worlds. With the help of human commerce, many gecko species have colonized areas of the world far from their homelands.

The 700-odd species of geckos occur on islands and continents. They may be found in sandy deserts, arid savannas, rocky steppes, areas of tidal wrack, tropical rain forests, and mountain-top cloud forests. They occur in suitable habitats from areas below sea level to elevations of nearly 2.5 miles.

Protected Types

With adaptations to so many habitats, it's not surprising that many gecko species are very common. A few are endangered. As of September 1994, only four species of geckos are listed threatened or endangered. These are:

• *Cyrtodactylus serpensinsula*, Serpent Island bent-toed gecko, Indian Ocean, Mauritius. Threatened.

• *Phelsuma edwardnewtoni*, Rodriguez day gecko, Rodriguez and surrounding

Threatened & Endangered Species

The statements made in this section are intended only as guidelines. Laws and regulations change regularly. Contact the appropriate regulatory agencies in your state, province, or country for current guidelines.

Various national and international treaties, regulations, and laws have been enacted to protect threatened and endangered (T&E) species. It is possible to legally acquire reptiles so designated, but it is difficult. Various permits from one or more regulatory agencies may be required. Before these permits are issued it will be necessary to complete substantial paperwork as well as to prove your expertise with the species in question. Permits applied for by zoological gardens and museums are rather routinely issued. Those applied for by private individuals are more carefully scrutinized.

In the United States (as of 1994), the federal government considers it legal to trade in legally held endangered or threatened species on an intrastate level without a permit. Interstate or international transportation of T&E species is legal without permit providing no commercial transaction (sale or trade) is involved. A permit is necessary if a commercial transaction is involved. State laws regarding T&E wildlife may also apply. Contact the nearest office of the United States Fish and Wildlife Service (Law Enforcement Division) and your state game and fish department to learn about current laws. If you reside in a country other than the United States, it will also be necessary to learn of, and to follow through on, the necessary permit processes.

islets. Last seen in 1917. Probably extinct, but officially designated as endangered.
• *Phelsuma guentheri*, Round Island day gecko, Round Island. Designated as endangered.

• *Sphaerodactylus micropithecus*, Monito gecko, Puerto Rico. Endangered.

Other species may be protected on state or local levels. It is mandatory that you learn of and obey federal, state, and local laws and regulations.

A profile of the rarely seen Naultinus grayi, *the New Zealand green gecko.*

Understanding Geckos

What Does Your Gecko Need?

A basic understanding of what a gecko needs in food and housing will go a long way toward helping you keep a pet gecko comfortable in captivity; in more technical terms, simulating natural conditions will help evoke natural behaviors in a captive specimen.

Identify Your Gecko

Start at the gecko's origin. With such a wide span in habitat—from lowland rain forests and deserts to cool, fog-shrouded mountaintops, to continents and islets, and from isolated wildernesses to urbanized areas—you'll need to know exactly what kind of gecko you have. The needs of a tokay (a persistently arboreal rain forest species) differ from the needs of a leopard gecko (a terrestrial desert species).

Where the lizard was found will help you determine what sort of habitat to provide, but you'll need to remember that several species have been transported by humans in produce and other goods to areas far away from their native lands. African, Asiatic, and European house geckos have become established halfway around the world in the southern United States, Mexico, and Central and South America. If your "source" for your pet gecko is the back wall of a dockside warehouse, you will need to make some inquiries to help you identify your species.

Housing

Perhaps 150 species are rather regularly seen in the pet trade. Of these a few are large species, 10 to14 inches (25.4–35.6 cm); most are of moderate size 4 to 7 inches (10.2–17.8 cm); and a few are tiny, 1.5 to 3.5 inches (3.8–8.9 cm). Knowing the adult size, along with home habitat, will help you in providing a comfortable and secure terrarium.

Cages for arboreal gecko species should be vertically oriented; those for terrestrial species should be horizontally oriented. Although desert geckos prefer low humidity in the cage, they may require somewhat more moisture in the sandy substrate. Tropical rain forest and woodland species require a higher overall humidity than desert and dry savanna forms. (See pages 23–25.)

What you provide in the way of decorative backdrop "furniture" in the terrarium may matter more to you than to the gecko. As long as your gecko has the perches, hiding areas, climbing surfaces, and warming areas it needs, it won't care what color scheme you choose.

Care and Feeding

Most geckos are nocturnal and insectivorous, ghosting over trees, rocks, or dwellings in pursuit of their insect prey on warm, still nights. A few geckos are omnivorous, consuming fruit, nectar, pollen, flower parts, and sweet saps besides the more usual insect prey. Geckos tend to be less active when the wind is blowing strongly or when the weather cools. House and wall geckos can often be seen around porch lights feeding on the insects drawn to the illumination. They may also bask in the warmth of the bulbs on cool evenings.

A few gecko species are diurnal. These day-active types include some of the most brilliantly colored members of the family—for example, many day geckos (*Phelsumas*).

As captives, geckos need warm temperatures (variable by species), live foods, and/or fruit-honey diets (variable by species); desert, woodland, rain forest, or savanna terrariums (also variable by species); and, as mentioned above, may be active by either day or night, or both. The techniques for providing water and lighting to geckos also vary—by gecko species, of course. In general, terrestrial geckos will often lap water from a dish or lap droplets from freshly misted substrate, whereas arboreal species often insist on drinking pendulous droplets from elevated positions such as leaves and limbs. (See page 26.)

How Long Will Your Gecko Live?

How long your gecko will live is very much an open-ended question. The life span of a captive gecko will depend upon numerous variables, which can be reduced to two items—the condition of the gecko when you received it (what was its age and health?) and the sort of care you give the lizard (is its life under your care better than it would have been in the wild?).

If properly cared for, even some of the smaller species can live for upward of five years. For instance, I have had specimens of the tiny yellow-tailed gecko (*Sphaerodactylus nigropunctatus flavicauda*), all adult when received, survive for more than six years as captives. Imported adult Bibron's geckos (*Pachydactylus bibroni*) regularly exceed a decade as captives. I have had a pair of Standing's day geckos, *Phelsuma standingi*, again fully adult when imported from Madagascar, for more

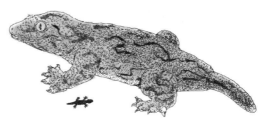

Comparative sizes of the largest and smallest geckos. Rhacodactylus leachianus *is almost ten times the length of* Lepidoblepharis sanctaemartae.

than 12 years, and they show no signs of slowing down yet.

How Big Are They?

The vast majority of the world's gecko species are between 4 and 7 inches (10.2–17.8 cm) in overall length—and about half that length is the tail. There are, of course, examples on both sides of that range. Let's consider the extremes.

The biggest: The largest gecko species yet known was designated as *Hoplodactylus delacourti*. Probably extinct, the single stuffed specimen of this hulking lizard measures 24.5 inches (62 cm) in overall length. Its point of origin is unknown, but because other members of the genus occur on New Zealand it is speculated that *H. delacourti* was (is?) from that region of the world.

At 14.5 inches (36.8 cm) from nose to tailtip, the New Caledonian giant gecko (*Rhacodactylus leachianus*) is now thought to be the world's largest living gecko. Other geckos approach or attain 1 foot (30.5 cm) in length. Among these are:

• Standing's day gecko (*Phelsuma standingi*) of Madagascar.
• Giant day gecko (*Phelsuma madagascariensis grandis*) of Madagascar.
• Tokay gecko (*Gekko gecko*) of tropi-

A handful of Rhacodactylus leachianus, *the giant New Caledonian gecko. This is the world's largest living gecko species.*

cal Asia (now introduced to other parts of the world).
• Green-eyed gecko (*Gekko stentor*) of Southeast Asia.
• Giant bent-toed gecko (*Cyrtodactylus biordinus*) of the Solomon Islands.

The smallest: The smallest geckos are the members of a New World subfamily, the Sphaerodactylinae. Of these, *Lepidoblepharis sanctaemartae* is the smallest, attaining a mere 1.5 inches (3.8 cm) in total length. Many of the reef and ashy geckos (genus *Sphaerodactylus*) are nearly as small, topping out at 2 to 3 inches (5.1–7.6) in total length.

Among the smallest of the Old World geckos are the 3-inch (7.6 cm) long members of the genus *Tropiocolotes*.

The Gecko's Eyes

The eyes of many gecko species are wonders to behold! Those of many nocturnal species bear wonderfully colored and intricately veined irides (irises) and strangely shaped, often scalloped, pupils. Conversely, the eyes of many diurnal forms are less ornate, of a dark color, and have rather "standard" round pupils.

Without lids: The eyes of the members of the family Gekkonidae (typical

---

Additional records of interest
• A Seychelles skin-sloughing gecko (*Ailuronyx seychellensis*) was maintained for more than six years by the Chaffee Zoological Gardens in Fresno, California. A wild-collected adult when received, it was still alive and healthy when disposed of.
• A male Namib sand gecko (*Chondrodactylus angulifer* ssp.) survived for almost 11 years at Woodland Park Zoo in Seattle.
• Mexican banded geckos (*Coleonyx e. elegans*) received as wild-collected adults have lived for more than 12 years as captives at both the Houston Zoological Gardens in Texas and in my collection.
• The somewhat smaller Tucson banded gecko (*C. variegatus bogerti*) has exceeded 15 years as a captive.

• Several records exist of leopard geckos (*Eublepharis macularius*) having lived for more than 20 years as captives. A similar life span is noted for numerous tokay geckos (*Gekko gecko*).
• Besides the Standing's day gecko, several congenerics have survived captivity for more than a decade. Among these are a Seychelles giant day gecko (*P. sundbergi*) in a private collection and a Round Island day gecko (*P. guentheri*) that was maintained by the Jersey Wildlife Preservation Trust in England.
• Even the greater frog-eyed gecko (*Teratoscincus scincus*), often thought of as a difficult captive, has survived in captivity for more than 12 years at the Fort Worth Zoo in Texas.

geckos) have no functional lids. Instead, the lids have fused, and a large transparent scale, the *brille* or spectacle, permanently covers and protects the eye. The brille is cleaned frequently by the broad, flat tongue of the gecko. (This same procedure is used by the eublepharine species that have fully functional lids and no protective brille.)

With lids: The members of the gecko family Eublepharidae (meaning "with eyelids") have fully functional eyelids. The species include the leopard and banded geckos and allies, all often collectively called eyelid or eublepharine geckos.

The pupils: The vertically elliptical pupils of the nocturnal geckos are remarkable in their diversity of shape. The pupils of the banded geckos are gently curved, those of the tokay have four gently curving scallops, and those of the giant Madagascan leaf-tailed gecko have more accentuated scal-

lops. When tightly contracted in bright light, the pupils appear as straight hairline slits, undulating waves that are equally thin, or as a series of two, three, or four pinpoints. The tight closure of the vertical pupil probably protects the light-sensitive retina of nocturnal forms from the sunlight as well as reducing glare, thus enhancing daylight vision. These would both be valid concerns for species that are wonderfully adapted for life in reduced-light situations.

The day and Old World dwarf geckos (genera *Phelsuma* and *Lygodactylus*), which are active by day, have round pupils that do not contract as tightly as those of the nocturnal species. Round pupils are also the hallmark of the diurnal and crepuscular yellow-headed geckos (and relatives) of the genus *Gonatodes*. However (and uncharacteristically), round pupils also are to be found in the tiny reef and ashy geckos (as well

Many geckos, (including Bibron's, seen here) have beautifully colored, intricately marked eyes.

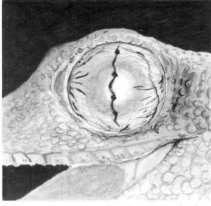

Most nocturnal geckos have vertical pupils that occur in a remarkably wide array of shapes.

as conspecifics of the genus *Sphaero-dactylus*), which are at least partially nocturnal.

At least as interesting as the pupils are the colors and venation in the irides of many nocturnal gecko species. Often the eye color is indistinguishable from the skin color. The patterns in the eye are so intricate that the lidless eyes of many species blend almost imperceptibly into the head and into background for which the gecko is best adapted (*Rhacodactylus* sp.). Others stand out in stark relief (*Palmatogecko rangei*). Golds, oranges, greens, and reds are the colors most frequently seen in geckos' eyes.

Eye structure: Rods and cones are abundant in the retina of many geckos. The abundance of these structures enhances both sight and color perception in both reduced- and strong-light situations. The retina also contains an abundance of nerve cells and fibers. Other gecko species lack the cones, having the retina packed with rods instead. These species have wonderfully acute sight in the darkness but no color perception.

The Gecko's Toes

Form follows function: The feet and toes of geckos are as varied as the purposes for which they have evolved. The webbed feet and expanded single digital pads of the flying geckos (*Ptychozoon* sp.) assist in both parachuting glides and secure climbing. The extensive webbing on the feet of the sand-adapted geckos *Palmatogecko rangei* (a species of the southwest African fog-deserts that is commonly known as the web-footed gecko) lack the expanded climbing lamellae, but the webs serve admirably as "snowshoes" and to enhance sand-swimming abilities. The toes of the sphere-toed geckos (genus *Sphaerodactylus*) terminate in a single rounded subdigital disk, whereas those of the leaf-toed geckos (genus *Phyllodactylus*) bear two expanded (leaflike) terminal subdigital pads. The house and turnip-tailed geckos (*Hemidactylus* and related genera, and *Thecadactylus*) bear a pair of elongated subdigital pads on each toe. The house geckos of the genus *Tarentola* have subdigital pads for the entire length of the toes.

Several gecko species lack all claws (*Crenadactylus ocellatus*, the clawless gecko) or some claws (*Chondrodactylus angulifer*, the South African sand gecko); several have retractile claws (the turnip-tailed gecko, *Thecadactylus rapicaudus*); others have the claws prominently fixed (flying geckos, *Ptychozoon* sp.).

The bent-toed geckos (*Cyrtodactylus* and related genera) are aptly named. Lacking even vestiges of expanded disks, the toes when viewed laterally are seen to be kinked and strongly clawed. Even though lacking subdigital pads, these geckos are fast and agile climbers on rocks and trees.

The common name of one species, the "lizard-fingered" gecko, is a literal translation of its scientific name,

Saurodactylus mauretanicus. This gecko has short toes that are not prominently kinked.

Some geckos lack both subdigital pads and kinks (the Caspian straight-fingered gecko, *Alsophylax pipiens*). Many sand dwellers have combs or serrate scales fringing their toes, which help them in moving over the shifting terrain.

Subdigital pads: What, exactly, are the subdigital pads and how do they work? The pads are made up of rows of transverse layers or lamellae (singular, lamella). These lamellae either grow as a single piece across the width of the toe or are divided medially. The lamellae contain tens of thousands of tiny hairlike structures called setae (singular, seta) each of which divides and terminates in several hundred (often) watchglass-shaped spatulae (singular, spatula). It is the grasping ability of these spatulae that gives a gecko its remarkable scansorial (climbing) abilities. Exactly how these microscopic spatulae grasp remains speculative. It is thought by some that these organs adhere to equally minute surface irregularities rather like microscopic suction cups. It is thought by others that the spatulae grip a surface by slipping into and around the irregularities. Still others have speculated that a buildup of static electricity may play a part in a gecko's clinging ability. Interestingly, it is not necessary for the gecko to be alive for the spatulae to grasp tightly to their support.

What's in a Tail?

Quick as a wink: Among lizards, many of which are notable for the ease with which they autotomize (drop) their tails, geckos are legendary. Some geckos will autotomize (drop) their tails with little more incentive than a mere brush by a keeper's or collector's hand or at the merest

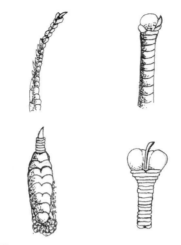

The subdigital pads of geckos vary from species to species.

touch of a predator. The autotomized tail wriggles convulsively, often drawing the attention of the "attacker" for a period of time sufficient to allow the now abbreviated lizard to escape. The tails then regenerate, but the regrown member often does not look at all like the original. Although the original tail is usually similar in scalation to the body and sleekly rounded, tapered, or flattened, regenerated tails may differ radically in scalation, may be bulbous and ungainly. If the break is unclean or partial, one, two, or even three tails may regenerate.

Some gecko species have derived both their common and scientific names from the appearance of a regenerated tail. One such is the Latin American turnip-tailed gecko, *Thecadactylus rapicaudus*.

Tail uses: Tails have several functions other than autotomizing and affording the gecko a chance to escape. The platelike scales on the dorsal surface of the tail of the greater frog-eyed gecko (*Teratoscincus s. scincus*) scrape together and make audible "chirps." The tail of the flying geckos of the genus *Ptychozoon* lend stability during the lizards' gliding flights. The tails of both Australian and Madagascan leaf-tailed geckos (genera *Phyllurus* and *Uroplatus*) are so flattened that they help the lizards blend imperceptibly into their tree-trunk backgrounds. The tails of leopard and fat-tailed geckos (*Eublepharis macularius* and *Hemitheconyx caudicinctus)* store fat in times of plenty. These reserves are then drawn on when prey is scarce or when weather conditions force inactivity.

The attractively whorled original tails of eublepharines are wriggled to and fro as the lizard prepares to pounce on its prey; however, the heavy and unattractive regenerated tails usually are not flexible enough for wriggling.

Some Australian diplodactyline geckos use their tails as burrow plugs. Other species of the same subfamily exude a sticky substance from specialized glands on the top of the tail; if

the gecko is extremely distressed, this syrupy substance may be forcibly discharged over a distance of 1 foot (30.5 cm) or more.

The tails of some geckos (*Lygodactylus* and others) have gripping lamellae at the tip similar to those on a gecko's toes and assist in climbing and holding a position. The tails of others (e.g., the New Zealand geckos of the genus *Naultinus*) are quite strongly prehensile. The canopy-dwelling members of the New Caledonian genus *Rhacodactylus* have tails that have clinging lamellae and are prehensile as well.

Tail language and function: Thus, we see that the tails of geckos are as diverse as the creatures themselves, and that a tail is not necessarily merely a tail. It may be "wagged" to indicate an excitement level, or may be used as a stopper, as an aid in climbing, or for any number of other purposes. In all cases, their tails are another example of the remarkable adaptations of these lizards.

Voice, Hearing and Smelling

Voice implies hearing: It would be counterproductive for a group of reptiles to be able to vocalize if others of their kind were not able to hear and respond to the sounds. Experimentation has shown that the hearing acuity of nocturnal geckos is well developed. The hearing ability of diurnal species may be somewhat less so.

Although many geckos of both the families Eublepharidae and Gekkonidae have voices, it would seem that all those of the subfamily Sphaerodactylinae are silent. The loud and frequent vocalizations of the Asian tokay (*Gekko gecko*) and the South African barking (also called "garrulous") geckos of the genus *Ptenopus* are well described. Other species click, squeak, squeal, and chuckle.

The South American turnip-tailed gecko, Thecadactylus rapicaudus, *is well camouflaged in its habitat.*

Although it is the males of most species that vocalize, the females of at least some are also able to produce sounds. In general, it is the males that vocalize messages of territoriality and aggression as well as sexual interest.

The nose knows: The sense of smell is also important to geckos. Not only do the paired Jacobson's organs inside the mouth seem to play a major role in scent identification, but geckos also seemingly nose around in an active effort to actually pick up tell-tale molecules. Watch your geckos explore their cage or a new territory. Often they pick specific sites to investigate, such as food dishes, egg-deposition sites and cagemates. Nose to task, they also use their tongues in exploring.

Glands on the tail of the Australian Diplodactylus ciliaris, *a spiny-tailed gecko, exude a viscous secretion.*

The Gecko Tongue

As a group, geckos have well-developed, long, broad, motile tongues that are slightly notched at the tip. The tongue is extended frequently and is used in many ways. It carries particles of scent into contact with the openings of the paired Jacobson's organs in the anterior palate. There the scents are analyzed. The tongue is also used in tasting objects, mostly to identify them for possible consumption. A gecko's sense of taste seems well developed. Captive day geckos, for instance, will consistently and preferentially choose the sweetest fruit-honey mixture from which to eat.

The tongue is also used to help determine the receptivity of potential breeding partners (by carrying pheromones—species-specific chemical stimulants—to the mouth), to help in the finding of suitable egg-deposition sites, and to clean the nose and eyes.

The Skin and Scales of Geckos

The protective skin: The skin of the gecko serves many functions, the most apparent of which is protection

of the delicate inner being from the harshness of the environment.

The skin can also play a significant part in the defense of the gecko. Certainly, by its color and texture the skin plays a major role in blending the gecko with its background. But there is more to the skin of the gecko, both in structure and function, than meets the eye.

The outermost skin: The outer layer of the gecko's skin, the epidermis, is composed of a material called keratin. Every scale—be it of the tiny granular type in which the yellow-headed gecko is clad, the enlarged (fish-like) variety of the frog-eyed gecko, or the prominently tuberculate, almost spiny, scales of the odd little African rough-scaled gecko—is merely a modified section of epidermis. The specialized transparent eyecaps of the eyelidless geckos are also composed of keratin. It is this outermost layer, the scaly covering, that is periodically shed (by all reptiles) and so is the most noticeable to us. The process of skin-shedding is technically known as *ecdysis*. It is from this keratinous outer layer of skin that the gecko derives its dry, "scaly" feel.

Geckos may shed their skins almost entirely or in a patchwork manner. To rid themselves of the exfoliating skin shards they may rub themselves against twigs, rocks, or other solid material, scratch the skin off with their claws, or contort and pull it off with their jaws. Many gecko species consume the skin as it is shed; other species do not.

The inner layer: Beneath the epidermis is the dermis. It is highly vascularized, contains connective tissue, bony, rigid "plates" called *osteoderms*, and pigment cells. Prismatic effects and the concentrations of the pigments within the cells at any given moment can be altered by nerve stimulation and/or hormonal activity. This accounts for both the perceived "standard" color as well as any color changes.

Structures in the skin: Although the skin of most lizards is largely free of glands, the femoral and preanal pores possessed by most gecko species and the secretion-expelling caudal (tail) glands of certain diplodactyline geckos are noteworthy exceptions.

The Endolymphatic ("Chalk") Sacs

Certain species of geckos of the subfamily Gekkoninae bear a large "chalk" or endolymphatic sac on each side of the neck. Members of the genus *Phelsuma* are one group that bear these sacs. Viewed from above, the sacs look like rounded bulges. Viewed from below, the white contents of calcium carbonate can usually be seen through the more translucent throat skin. The role of the sacs has not been determined, but there are several interesting theories.

Egg Laying: The sacs are largest on the females, and are especially prominent during eggshell formation. It has been suggested that these calcium deposits are the main source for the eggshell material. This theory is lent credence by the facts that the sacs increase in size during the reproductive season and that only the members of the Gekkoninae, a subfamily that lays hard-shelled eggs, have the sacs.

Calcium metabolism: The fact that the males also possess the sacs detracts somewhat from the egg-laying theory. This suggests that the sacs are used in calcium metabolism.

Equilibrium: Another theory is that the sacs are static balance organs. This would help account for their presence in both sexes. In time, more will be known about the role(s) and value(s) of these organs.

Gecko Behavior

Because of the several very different lifestyles embraced by the various geckos, it is difficult to generalize on understanding these lizards. For particulars, read the chapters in which I have discussed geckos as behavioral groups as well as the individual species accounts. In each I have mentioned individual peculiarities.

There are, however, a few rather standardized mannerisms and needs of the geckos as a lizard group.

• Although most female geckos will rather peacefully coexist with others of their own species and sex, sexually mature males of the same (or closely allied) species will fight savagely with others of their sex. Sexually mature geckos of all species are best housed in pairs or trios (one male and two females). Visual barriers (branches, hollow logs, hide boxes) in a cage (or even between cages) will be appreciated by all.

• Antagonism and unease between male geckos will be manifested by rapid head bobs and lateral nods.

Pursuit and actual skirmishing will rapidly follow. Males in closely allied species groups (e.g., giant day and Standing's day geckos) will fight as persistently as males of the same species group. However, head bobbing and nodding may also indicate courtship when used by a male in the presence of a female.

• Tail wagging and writhing may indicate nervousness (when used in the presence of geckos of the same sex), have sexual overtones (when used in the presence of geckos of the opposite sex), or indicate an interest in a prey item (when employed by a hungry, hunting gecko).

• Of the two gecko groups, the members of the eyelid geckos (leopard, fat-tailed) seem to resent handling less than most of the true geckos. The skin of all is easily torn but the skin of the day

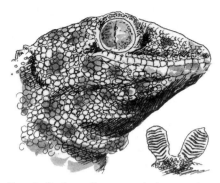

Due to its broadly expanded toepads, the agressive tokay gecko is able to climb vertical glass panels with ease.

geckos and the skin-sloughing gecko is especially delicate. As a generality, geckos should be considered display lizards that should not be handled.

Enlarged endolymphatic sacs are apparent on the neck of this adult female Standing's day gecko, Phelsuma standingi. *She is in a typical head-down stance.*

Housing, Care, and Management

For arboreal geckos, the height of the terrarium provided should be of as much consideration as the floor space. If it is terrestrial geckos that you are housing, then, of course, the height of the cage is far less important.

There are four types of terrariums that may be considered. All can have both terrestrial and arboreal applications.

Basic Caging

Whereas elaborately planted terrariums are the norm among European herpetoculturists, many American hobbyists prefer cages that are both basic in design and simplicity. Such basic caging can be adapted from premade aquariums (the all-glass types serve well in this capacity and are readily available in many sizes) or can be built (by handymen or cabinetmakers) from wood and glass, or in some cases wood and wire.

When terrariums/cages are built, I have found it a good idea to incorporate large casters into their design so that they may be easily moved about. This is especially handy when large terrariums/cages are involved. In warm climates, where many gecko species can remain outdoors for most or all of the year, I have successfully used large "step-in" caging for many arboreal species. Those that I use have cage dimensions of 66 (height) × 48 (length) × 30 (width) inches (167.6 × 121.9 × 76.2 cm). The frames are made of 2 × 2 inch (5.1 × 5.1 cm) lumber, the base is from 0.75 inch (19

mm) marine plywood, and the wire is 0.125-inch (3.2 mm) mesh hardware cloth. The small mesh of the wire assures that all but the smallest feed crickets will remain within the cage. When placed on casters, the overall height is elevated to 71 inches (180.3 cm), which allows the cages to be rolled indoors (through sliding patio doors) if it does become necessary. If left outdoors during cool weather, the cages are wrapped in clear 4 mil vinyl or polyethylene. This is stapled in place on three sides, but can be rolled up and out of the way or removed from the top and south side (door side) if desired. A heat lamp is activated when necessary. To assure the comfort of the lizards, except for the removable front and top, the plastic sheeting can (and probably should) remain in place throughout the winter months. The geckos spend hours hanging on the sunny uprights of the frame or may leisurely bask on the horizontals of the door frame. The bottom can be left bare or a low frame can be installed that will retain a clean sand substrate. (Although I do use sand on the bottoms of my cages, I merely pile it high in the cage center and let it seek its own level—including being washed out—during storms.) I also utilize hardy potted plants (cycads or ficus) within the cages. These serve the dual purposes of decoration and providing visual barriers. Within these cages, many types of day geckos, tokays, and related species have successfully bred.

A simple glass and wood box will house almost all species of geckos in comfort.

A glass aquarium standing on its short end can be adapted to provide a good enclosure for arboreal geckos.

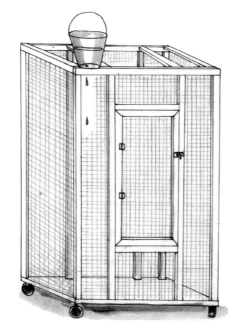

A rolling "walk-in" cage of wire mesh and wood works well for outdoor use.

The actual dimensions of cages such as these can vary according to your individual needs. I do suggest, however, that you never construct them so large that they cannot be easily rolled through both interior and exterior doors.

Using an Aquarium/Terrarium

The glass terrarium can be oriented in the standard ("top-up") position for terrestrial gecko species, or positioned in an upright position for arboreal species. A suitable top (or front, as the case may be) will need to be provided. With the standard orientation this poses no problem. However, when the upright orientation is preferred, formulating an escape-proof front becomes more difficult. This may be approached from two angles. Firstly, if not too heavy, a glass front may be cut and held in position with a hinge of Silastic aquarium sealant. A hook and hasp may be similarly held in place on the opposite side. I have found that if the edge of the glass door rests flush against the table or stand top (or the inside glass of the terrarium), the sealant hinge is much less stressed. The second method is to set your terrarium 1 to 2 inches (2.5–5.1 cm) off of the flat surface on blocks or legs. A tightly fitting framed front can then be merely slipped over the open side (if this is divided in half, it will be easier to restrain nervous specimens).

Desert Terrarium

Many terrestrial and rock-dwelling (saxicolous) gecko species are desert dwellers. These, of course, survive best if provided with a terrarium simulating a desert habitat. Like the basic cage, this can be as large or as small, as complex or as simple, as prudence dictates. The sizes and activity patterns of your specimens should always be carefully considered.

The Substrate: Although many herpetoculturists caution against the use of sand as a substrate (citing intestinal impactions if it is ingested by the gecko inhabitants), I have always used it successfully. In more than 40 years of gecko keeping I have never lost a single specimen to impaction, and, after all, what is a desert if not sand? However, if the chance of sand-related problems does worry you, the use of smooth, variably sized rocks can also be considered. Here I would caution against the use of sharp-sided silica aquarium gravel; if accidentally ingested by your specimens it could be of more potential danger than the finer builder's sand.

The depth of the substrate can vary. If only a fine covering is used, your tank will, of course, be lighter and easier to move and handle. If a thick layer of substrate is used, you will be able to better maintain the barely dampened bottom layer and the dry top layer preferred by some gecko species. Rock ledges and caves, individual basking rocks, potted arid-land

A terrarium for a desert gecko species. Heat and light, water, and hiding areas must be provided. The humidity should be kept low.

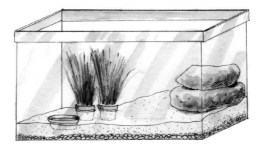

With the addition of grassy plants you can create a savanna terrarium.

A slightly more elaborate terrarium for woodland gecko species uses leaf cover, climbing plants, and hiding areas.

plants, cork bark hiding areas, and cholla cactus skeletons can be provided both for decoration and the psychological well-being of your specimen(s). Because most desert-dwelling reptiles are adapted to low humidity, the top of your desert terrarium should be of screen. This will prevent a buildup of internal humidity that could be detrimental to the health of your lizard.

Savanna Terrarium

Savannas are areas of transition between or at the edge of forest, woodland, or desert. Spacious, rolling glades, these (often) sparsely vegetated areas are the habitats of many gecko species. Different soil formation and moderate rainfall provide a habitat much different from that of either surrounding desert or woodland and forest. Savannas often host various species of moderately, or at least seasonally, lush grasses, as well as thornscrub and other formidably armed trees. Areas of rocky scree may be present.

Savannas are often subjected to weather extremes in the form of temperature, rainfall, or other such climatic vagaries. The plant community found in savannas is difficult to maintain in terrariums over extended periods. Periodic refurbishing of your terrarium vegetation will most likely be necessary.

The substrate: A thick layer of sandy humus into which a liberal helping of variably sized rocks has been mixed should comprise the substrate of the savanna terrarium. Seedling acacias and clumped grasses, as well as weathered branches, cactus skeletons, and strategically placed rocks and rock formations can be used for decorative purposes. The savanna terrarium plant community will require somewhat more water than those in the desert terrarium. However, even

with judicious care, many (especially the grasses) will need replacing each season. The plants can be either potted or planted directly into the terrarium substrate. I prefer the latter, for many gecko species enjoy digging their burrows into and beneath the plant's root systems. A screen top will assist you in keeping the low humidity preferred by most savanna-dwelling gecko species.

Woodland and Forest Terrariums

Woodland and forest terrariums can be utilized for those geckos of humid, rainy temperate and tropical origins. Because of the host of easily grown potted houseplants and scientifically formulated soils that are available, woodland and forest terrariums are among the most easily constructed and maintained of the various terrarium types. Besides, the plants, attractive branches and rocks work well as decorative and functional objects in the woodland and forest terrariums. To successfully maintain your plants, it will be necessary to assure that their roots remain damp, but not soggy, and to provide them with adequate lighting. Even shade-tolerant philodendrons, pothos, and syngoniums will require several hours of fairly strong light daily if they are to survive.

The substrate: When constructing a woodland terrarium, I suggest first placing 1 to 2 inches (2.5–5.1 cm) of pea-sized gravel as the base of the substrate. Atop this I lay a thickness or two of air-conditioning filter material cut to the exact size of the terrarium. This latter prevents the 2 to 3 inches (5.1–7.6 cm) of soil that comes next from filling the spaces between the gravel. The rocks below the air-conditioning filters act as a reservoir that will prevent excess water from destroying the roots of your plants if you should happen to overwater.

The plate-like scales on the tail of the greater frog-eyed gecko (seen here in a savanna terrarium), can produce a rasping noise when the tail is writhed.

Of course, if you regularly overwater, the reservoir will become filled and provide little benefit to the setup. A glass or plastic top will help retain the high humidity preferred by many of the denizens of these habitats. If the humidity remains too high it can be reduced by substituting a screen, or a combination screen and glass cover, for the full glass one.

HOW-TO:
Watering Techniques

Water Dishes

Some arboreal geckos will lap water from dishes in elevated positions (so that they may drink without going onto the ground). This is especially so if the surface of the water is roiled by a bubbling aquarium air stone.

Many but not all terrestrial geckos will lap water from dishes. If your specimens are reluctant to drink still water, the technique of roiling the water surface with a bubbling aquarium air stone will usually solve the problem.

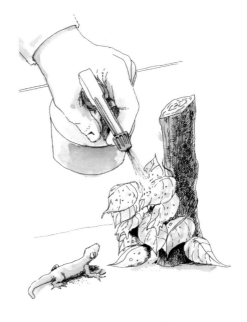

Some arboreal geckos need an elevated water dish.

Ground-dwelling species may drink if the surface of the water is roiled.

Misting

Not all geckos will use water dishes. This is especially true of persistently arboreal species, which in nature lap dew and raindrops from leaves and limbs. Gently misting your terrarium (until pendulous droplets form on leaves and perches) is the most suitable way of providing water for your arboreal geckos. Do this daily.

Hydration Chamber

The uses and benefits of hydration chambers have long been appreciated by zoos and other public institutions. They are only now coming into general use by private herpetoculturists and hobbyists. The term hydration chamber is merely an overstated way of saying rain chamber. But there is nothing overstated about the rain chamber's value to the herpetoculturist. These receptacles can make the difference between life and death for

Use a sprayer to mist water onto leaf surfaces.

Droplets from leaves also increase humidity within the enclosure.

dehydrated lizards (or any other reptiles or amphibians).

Making your own: A hydration chamber can be constructed of wire mesh over a wood frame, or of an aquarium equipped with a circulating water pump and a screen or perforated Plexiglas top. If you are fortunate enough to live in a benign climate where the cage can be placed outdoors, a mist nozzle can be placed on the end of a hose and affixed over the cage, and fresh water run through this for an hour or more a day. (If your community chlorinates or adds chloramines to the water supply, the "mist nozzle" technique can be detrimental to amphibians, all of which have permeable skins. Treated water is less problematic for reptiles.)

If indoors, the cage can be placed on top or inside of a properly drained utility tub and the fresh water system used. It is imperative that the drain system be adequate and kept free of debris if this system is used indoors. A secondary (back-up) drain (just in case) might do much to guarantee your peace of mind.

In contained systems, the circulation pump forces water from the tank itself through a small diameter PVC pipe into which a series of lateral holes has been drilled, or merely brought up to the top of the tank and allowed to drip through the screen or perforated Plexiglas. It is imperative that the water in self-contained systems be kept immaculately clean.

Why use a chamber? The use of these (or similar) units can do much to help moisture-starved reptiles recuperate. Those that will most benefit from such a structure are the rainforest species that are shipped long distances to reach the pet markets of America, Asia, Europe, and other countries. Among others, the various Madagascar leaf-tailed geckos and rain forest species of bent-toed geckos are prime candidates for hydration chamber treatment. Desert species will rarely if ever need this sort of treatment.

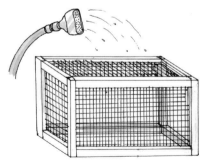

Even a simple hydration chamber provides a life-replenishing "rest stop" for dehydrated geckos.

Captive breeding of Oedura castelnaui, *the northern velvet gecko, has made the lizard widely available. This species will do well in a rocky savanna terrarium.*

Choosing Cage Furnishings

Cage furnishings for geckos can be either primarily functional or, more usually, both functional and decorative. Among the primarily functional examples are such items as "hot rocks" and heating "limbs." Rock formations and caves that provide both beauty and a hiding area for your geckos, or sturdy-leafed plants and limbs that provide both perches and visual barriers as well as adding beauty to the terrarium, are perfect examples of the "dual purpose" cage furnishings.

Rocks: If multilayered rock formations or caves are provided, the rocks should be held in place (and together) with a nontoxic adhesive. Latex aquarium sealant is quite satisfactory for this purpose. If even a single flat rock is placed on the surface of the sand, it should be ascertained that it cannot shift and injure your gecko should your pet burrow beneath it. Natural rocks provide better

clawholds for your specimens than do the decorative glassrocks.

Wood: Bleached manzanita and other gnarled woods are often available at pet shops or from the wild. These provide perches and visual barriers for terrarium inhabitants.

Cork bark comes in many shapes and sizes. It is available in small tubes into which shy geckos can retire if they choose, or in curved lengths, which can provide lightweight caves when laid atop the terrarium's substrate.

Plants of many types are readily available and serve many purposes when placed in a terrarium. As mentioned earlier, stiff-leafed types such as sansevierias or aloes can serve as both perches and visual barriers. Additionally, some gecko species like to place their eggs in the basal rosette of sansieveria leaves. If misted, the leaves of these (or any other) plants can provide drinking stations for your geckos.

Naultinus grayi, *the New Zealand green gecko, is one of the few live-bearing gecko species.*

The curved cedar hideboxes so often seen in pet shops are *not* satisfactory for use with reptiles. Cedar contains resins that are detrimental to the health of reptiles.

Terrarium Cleanliness

Terrarium cleanliness is one of the most important aspects of successful gecko husbandry. The substrate should be changed or washed frequently, the perches should be scraped and washed as necessary, and all hard surfaces, such as rocks and glass, should be cleaned and sterilized. Water, whether in bowls or daily mists, *must* be fresh and clean.

Fortunately, geckos are relatively small lizards, and they aren't sloppy feeders like varanids. Keeping a gecko cage clean is usually rather easy. Terrestrial geckos usually choose a corner of their tank in which to defecate, so this area will need to be changed more frequently than the rest of the substrate. Similarly, arboreal geckos may choose a particular perch or a corner as their stooling area. Again, these areas will need frequent cleaning.

If you are using a sand substrate, it can be washed, sterilized, dried, and reused. Dirty wood chips or mulch should be discarded and new ones used. To sterilize sand, perches, twigs, rocks, cork bark, cholla skeletons, and the terrarium itself, a diluted solution of either Ro-Cal or chlorine bleach should be used. After cleaning and sterilizing the items, be sure all are thoroughly rinsed with clean, fresh water.

Terrarium cleanliness will do much to assure the long-term good health of your geckos. Regular cleaning will help prevent the spread of both diseases and endoparasites. The cleaning of terrariums should be a prominent part of your husbandry regimen.

My tip: Do not use pine oils or other phenol-based disinfectants for cleaning reptile and amphibian cages. Phenols are not tolerated well by reptiles. Even lingering odors can be deleterious.

HOW-TO:
Lighting and Heating

Heating Your Terrarium

The way you should provide heat to your geckos will depend on the habits of the species of gecko involved. Fortunately, many heat sources are available today that were not even thought about a decade ago. Among these are "hot rocks," "heating branches," under-tank heaters, "sub-sand" heating pads, heat tapes, ceramic heating units that screw into regular bulb fixtures, and, of course, heat bulbs. Many of these implements are thermostatically controlled, others are of low wattage, hence low heat, but some may require that a rheostat or thermometer be incorporated into the circuitry by the purchaser.

Here are some facts that should be considered.

When it comes to thermoregulation, geckos embrace three lifestyles:

• Heliothermic (sun-basking, day-active species).

• Thigmothermic species (those that thermoregulate by lying on or against a previously warmed object such as a rock, tree limb, or even a road surface). Most nocturnal geckos are thigmotherms.

• Those that live in geographic areas so ideal that little additional warming is necessary.

For heliotherms a heat lamp is ideal. Basking surface temperatures of between 88 and 94°F (31.1–34.4°C) are suit-

able. It would seem that overhead lighting is as necessary for the psychological well-being of these species as for the warmth provided. If the animals are agonistic (antagonistic toward each other), more than a single basking area may need to be provided. In any event, be sure to provide a thermal gradient (warm to cool). Cooler areas to which the specimen(s) can retire if necessary are mandatory. (Refer to Species Accounts, beginning page 46 for individual species particulars.)

Many sources of supplementary heat are available for thigmotherms. Among these are the various hot rocks, heat limbs, under-tank heaters, and heat tapes. Of all, I prefer the under-tank heaters for terrestrial geckos. The hot rocks have not only been known to malfunction (overheating and burning the specimens that use them); they can be difficult to keep clean of feces and uric acid, as well. The newly available heat limbs or branches seem ideal for many nocturnal arboreal

geckos. Many under-tank heaters are thermostatically controlled. Some herpetoculturists build a back-up thermostat into the unit as a safeguard. Only a part (one-half or slightly less) of the tank should be heated. This will allow a thermal gradient within the terrarium that your gecko will appreciate and use to advantage.

Lighting Your Terrarium

Is "full-spectrum" lighting necessary for your gecko? The role of full-spectrum lighting in gecko husbandry is poorly understood. It would seem that full-spectrum lighting would be less necessary for the nocturnal forms than it would for diurnal species. It has been rather conclusively shown that light rays in the ultraviolet (UV) spectrum are beneficial to all basking reptiles. The emissions in the UV-A bands promote natural behavior in reptiles, whereas those in the UV-B lengths have been shown to enhance the synthesis of vitamin D_3. Vitamin D_3, in turn, enhances the absorption of calcium. Without full-spectrum

With the wide variety of lighting available—from full-spectrum UV incandescent bulbs, to ordinary incandescent bulbs to heat lamps—you can simulate natural light and provide basking areas for your geckos.

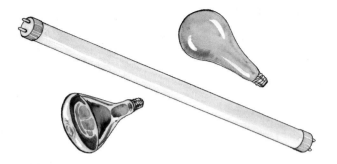

UV incandescent, full-spectrum fluorescent, and heat lamps are available at most pet and hardware stores.

lighting, dietary augmentation with D$_3$ and calcium is necessary on a frequent basis (these should be provided in greatest quantity to gravid females and rapidly growing juveniles). With full-spectrum lighting the dietary augmentations can be less frequent. Without vitamin D$_3$, calcium is only poorly metabolized by reptiles.

Natural unfiltered sunlight remains the best full-spectrum lighting available. In southern Florida, I am able to leave my caging outdoors year-round. The wood and wire cage construction allows the day geckos to bask at will in unfiltered sunshine. On cool winter days, even some of the nocturnal species may bask, although they are probably partaking of the warmth provided rather then the sunlight itself. In passing through most types of glass and Plexiglas, the beneficial rays normally provided by sunlight are filtered out. Care should be taken that glass terrariums are *not* placed outdoors in the full sunlight. The glass of the terrarium will concentrate the heat

and quickly kill even the most heat-tolerant of reptiles.

The most satisfactory artificial full-spectrum emissions seem to be provided by several brands of fluorescent tubes specifically designated "full-spectrum." Incandescent bulbs claimed to be full-spectrum are now making an appearance; the efficiency of these needs to be carefully evaluated and compared with the fluorescent types. Although "plant-grow" bulbs are *not* full-spectrum, I find them ideal for enhancing the growth of live plants in the terrarium. Additionally, if their warmth is directed to a basking perch or other such area, these bulbs can provide a suitable "hot spot" in which diurnal geckos may bask. Warm basking areas can be provided equally well by "regular" incandescent flood bulbs, but these are not as effective for inducing plant growth.

In overview, using full-spectrum fluorescent tubes in conjunction with incandescent lighting will provide the best overall benefits for indoor terrariums.

Avoiding Electrical Accidents

It is important to use caution when handling electrical equipment and wiring, which are particularly hazardous when used in connection with water. Always observe the following safeguards carefully:

• Before using any of the electrical equipment described in this book, check to be sure that it carries the UL symbol.

• Keep all lamps away from water or spray.

• Before using any equipment in water, check the label to make sure it is suitable for underwater use.

• Disconnect the main electrical plug before you begin any work in a water terrarium or touch any equipment.

• Be sure that the electric current you use passes through a central fuse box or circuit-breaker system. Such a system should be installed only by a licensed electrician.

Your Gecko's Health

Choosing a Healthy Gecko

When you are ready to purchase a gecko, start by selecting a well-run pet store in which the animals are displayed in clean, roomy, well-lighted enclosures. Then, spend some time observing the specimens. When you are ready to choose a gecko, it is very important that you choose a healthy one. Ascertaining good health may not be quite as easily accomplished with geckos as with some other lizards. With reptiles in general, there are a few cues that signal "caution" when choosing a pet. These rules change slightly when applied to geckos, especially those that apply to basic demeanor, alertness, and color.

My tip: Geckos are secretive and quiet lizards that often cling tightly to a branch, rock, or whatever upon which they are sitting. This quietness may make them seem less alert. But there is another factor to consider when it comes to alertness. Many people seem to find it easier to judge the condition of geckos with eyelids; those geckos seem more alert. If you compare geckos without eyelids, like the tokays, to geckos with eyelids (the leopards and fat-tails), you'll note the geckos with eyelids just seem to be more aware of what's going on around them.

Eyes: When choosing a gecko, you do not normally choose one with sunken eyes. But the eyes of a perfectly healthy typical gecko may appear sunken when the lizard is sleeping. Thus, the eyes of sleeping *and* unhealthy geckos may appear sunken. However, if the individual is only sleeping, the eyes will take on a normal outline once the lizard awakens and begins moving.

Coloration: Color can also be a cue to health, but don't act in haste. A frightened gecko will often assume the darker hues usually associated with unhealthy specimens. Again, if left undisturbed for a few minutes, the lizard's normal brilliance should return.

Weight: Look at the overall size and body weight of the gecko. Although some gecko species are normally very slender, neither pelvis nor ribs should be prominently apparent. A protruding pelvis or "accordion" ribs indicate an unnatural thinness that may be associated with improper diet, dehydration, parasitism, or other problems. Reversing this problem may not be possible; like most reptiles, geckos are slow to show illness until it is far advanced.

Until you become familiar with the creatures, when choosing a gecko it is always best if you take a knowledgeable person—one who knows geckos—with you. Many species are normally hardy, some are normally delicate, but you will have a better chance with all if you start off with a healthy example.

My tip: When choosing a gecko, select one with typical color, good ("normal") body weight, and eyes that are not sunken or dull. Choose one that moves quickly and alertly when it is disturbed. If in a communal terrarium and all but one gecko dart quickly away when disturbed, *do not* choose the one that remains quiescent. This is more apt to be a sign of ill health than of tolerance.

Caution: Be careful when you handle a gecko. Remember, the skin of many geckos will tear readily if the lizards are grasped. This is especially true of the phelsumas. You simply cannot handle these little lizards at all. Having the fragile integument tear under your grasp is very disconcerting for you and more traumatic for the lizard.

If given good care, geckos are wonderful and usually long-lived lizards. If you choose yours carefully the chances are that you will become a satisfied hobbyist.

Skin Shedding

How Frequently Will My Gecko Shed?

The growth rate and overall health of your specimen will have much to do with the frequency with which it sheds its skin. The process results from thyroid activity. A day or two prior to shedding, the colors of your gecko will appear to fade. As the old keratinous layer loosens from the new one forming beneath it, your gecko may take on an overall grayish or silvery sheen. When shedding has been completed, your specimen will again be brightly marked as it was to begin with.

Problems in Shedding

Although it seems that wild geckos seldom have problems shedding, some captives may. Shedding problems may often be associated with newly imported lizards, those that are dehydrated or in otherwise suboptimal condition, or when the relative humidity in the gecko terrarium/cage is too low. Shedding problems are most often associated with toes and tail tips where, if not then manually (and *very* carefully) removed by the keeper, their adherence and drying in place can result in toe or tail tip loss. If patches of skin adhere, a gentle misting with

tepid water may help your gecko rid itself of the pieces.

Safe Handling

Do's and don'ts: Most geckos should be considered display animals only. That is, they should be watched and appreciated but not handled. This is especially true of those whose skin tears easily (*Phelsuma, Ailuronyx, Teratoscincus*) or whose tails autotomize almost voluntarily (*Teratoscincus*). It is best to shepherd those species into a cardboard tube, jar, glass, or other such receptacle rather than manually grasp them. Indeed, the skin of *Ailuronyx seychellensis* is so easily

Although most day geckos will not crawl onto your hand, should one do so, keep your hand flat and motionless until the lizard crawls off.

torn that it has been given the common name of "skin-sloughing gecko." Some geckos (*Gekko gecko* and *Gekko stentor*, among others) can and will bite a hand painfully hard if carelessly restrained.

Cautions: Even such relatively easy-to-handle specimens as leopard and fat-tailed geckos do not like to be grasped. However, these species will often crawl rather confidently into your hand where they can then be gently cupped with the other hand. It is important that terrestrial geckos not be allowed to crawl out of your hand and drop to the ground. Such a drop can result in internal damage, broken limbs, and/or autotomized tail. Although arboreal species, which are more adapted to jumping, dropping, or actually falling, may suffer less from accidental falls, they still should not be handled carelessly.

Gecko fears: Geckos are alert lizards that usually perceive an approaching hand as having predatory intentions and will dart away quickly as the hand nears. I feel that you should honor the reluctance of these lizards to be handled. Handling your geckos little and providing them with surroundings in which they feel secure will promote good health and perhaps even be an important prelude to successful breeding programs.

Quarantine

To prevent the spread of diseases and parasites between geckos, it is important that you quarantine new specimens for a given period of time, of at least a week. This means that the lizard should be in a cage by itself, and that you make sure you do not transmit any possible pathogens by washing your hands before and after you clean its cage, change its water, or examine the lizard itself. During quarantine, take the time just to watch your lizard. During this time, fecal exams should be carried out to determine whether or not endoparasites are present. For this, you simply take a stool specimen to your reptile veterinarian. The quarantine area should be completely removed from the area in which other reptiles are kept—preferably in another room.

The quarantine tank should be thoroughly cleaned prior to the introduction of the new lizard(s) and it should be regularly cleaned throughout the quarantine period. As with any other terrarium, the quarantine tank should be geared to the needs of the specimen that it is to house. Temperature, humidity, size, lighting, and all other factors must be considered.

Only after you (and your veterinarian) are completely satisfied that your new specimen(s) are healthy and habituated should they be brought near other specimens.

My tip: This quarantine period can be one of the most important periods in the life of your gecko. You will then be able to notice most health problems, be they established or incipient. Feeding regimens can also be established, and your specimen can become at least semi-accustomed to the presence of people near its quarters. The importance of quarantine should not be overlooked and cannot be overemphasized!

Important: Reptilian veterinary medicine is a specialized field. Not every veterinarian is qualified. It is most important to find a qualified veterinarian before you actually need the services of one.

Parasites

Many geckos, even those that are captive-bred and hatched, may harbor internal parasites. Because of the complexities of identification of endoparasites and the necessity to accurately weigh specimens to be treated and measure purge dosages, the eradication of internal parasites is best left to a qualified reptile veterinarian. It is important to use the correct medications and correct dosages, especially because geckos are such small creatures; there is no room for error. These are a few of the recommended medications and dosages, each keyed to a specific parasite. Dosages are courtesy of Richard Funk, D.V.M.

Amoebas and trichomonads:
40–50 mg/kg of Metronidazole orally. The treatment is repeated in two weeks.

Dimetridazole can also be used but the dosage is very different. 40–50 mg/kg of Dimetridazole is administered daily for five days. The treatment is then repeated in two weeks. All treatments with both medications are administered once daily.

Coccidia: Many treatments are available.

The dosages of sulfadiazine, sulfamerazine, and sulfamethazine are identical. Administer 75 mg/kg the first day, then follow up for the next five days with 45 mg/kg. All treatments should be given orally and once daily.

Sulfadimethoxine is also effective. The initial dosage is 90 mg/kg orally to be followed on the next five days with 45 mg/kg orally. All dosages are administered once daily.

Trimethoprim-sulfa may also be used. 30 mg/kg should be administered once daily for seven days.

Cestodes (Tapeworms): Several effective treatments are available.

Bunamidine may be administered orally at a dosage of 50 mg/kg. A second treatment occurs in 14 days.

Niclosamide, orally, at a dosage of 150 mg/kg, is also effective. A second treatment is given in two weeks.

Praziquantel may be administered either orally or intramuscularly. The dosage is 5-8 mg/kg and is to be repeated in 14 days.

Trematodes (Flukes):
Praziquantel at 8 mg/kg may be administered either orally or intramuscularly. The treatment is repeated in two weeks.

Nematodes (roundworms):
Several effective treatments are available.

Levamisole, an injectible intraperitoneal treatment, should be administered at a dosage of 10 mg/kg and the treatment repeated in two weeks.

Ivermectin, injected intramuscularly in a dosage of 200 mcg/kg is effective. The treatment is to be repeated in two weeks. Ivermectin can be toxic to certain taxa.

Thiabendazole and fenbendazole have similar dosages. Both are administered orally at 50–100 mg/kg and repeated in 14 days.

Mebendazole is administered orally at a dosage of 20–25 mg/kg and repeated in 14 days.

Medical Abbreviations
mg = milligram
(1 mg = 0.001 gram)
kg = kilogram
(1000 grams; 2.2 pounds)
mcg = microgram
(1 mcg = 0.000001 gram)
IM = intramuscularly
IP = intraperitoneally
PO = orally

Diets

Getting Started

Although most geckos are basically insectivorous, some larger species will also prey on the nestlings of mice and small birds. Additionally, many lap a goodly amount of pollen, nectar, sweet tree saps, and exudate from soft, overripe fruit. Finding out your gecko's dietary habits is easily done once you know what kind you have. The real work may be in persuading the lizard to feed. Once deprived of food and water (for instance, at the wholesaler who is less than careful about feeding and hygiene), some geckos just don't want to get started again. It will be your responsibility to offer fresh food in such secure and calming surroundings that your gecko just cannot resist maybe just nibbling, then readily feeding. It can be quite a task, but the life of your gecko depends on it.

Insects

Insect care: So your gecko likes insects—what could be easier? Like other things, there's more to feeding insects than tossing a few odd crickets into the cage. You've got to feed your insects well before your offer them to your geckos. This sort of caring properly for your feed insects is an important aspect of successful herpetological husbandry. A poorly fed or otherwise unhealthy insect offers little but bulk when fed to a reptile or amphibian. You may watch your geckos eat feed insects every day, yet if the insects are not healthy, your geckos may be slowly starving. Thus, maintaining your insects in top-notch health should be a main concern of any herpetoculturist.

A sweep net for gathering field plankton.

Feeding insects: Before mentioning specific care for several of the more commonly used food insects, I feel that a mention of "gut-loading" is in order. In this technique your insects are fed an abundance of highly nutritious foods immediately before being offered as food to your geckos. Calcium, vitamin D_3, fresh fruit and vegetables, fresh alfalfa and/or bean sprouts, and honey and vitamin-mineral enhanced (chick) laying mash are only a few of the foods that may be considered for gut-loading insects. A commercially prepared gut-loading diet has only recently reached the pet marketplace. Insects quickly lose much of their food value if not continually fed an abundance of highly nourishing foodstuffs. Most insects eat rather continually, so it is much to the benefit of your lizards if you supply the insects with the highest possible quality diet.

Except for field plankton, all feed insects, even houseflies, are commercially available. It may be your preference to avail yourself regularly of the various commercial sources. Certainly this is less time-consuming than breeding your own insects. However, by breeding your own you can assure that the best possible diet is continually fed the insects. Even if procuring the insects commercially, you should begin feeding them the best diet possible as soon as you receive them.

Field plankton

Insects straight "from the wild" are already well fed. These insects have been able to choose their diet and their nutritive value reflects this. Perhaps the very best diet that you can supply your geckos is that known colloquially as field plankton or field mixture. This is merely a mixture of the various insects and other arthropods that can be field-collected in any given location. To gather them, you simply sweep a suitably meshed field net back and forth through tall grasses or low shrubs after first ascertaining that the area is chemical free.

Having fed on natural, native foods, these insects are probably at their pinnacle of health. Fed to your geckos immediately after collecting, the insects, with their good health and full guts, will greatly benefit the lizards.

Crickets

The gray cricket (*Acheta domesticus*), is now bred commercially by the millions both for fishing bait and for pet food. Other species are readily collected in small numbers beneath debris in fields, meadows, and open woodlands. If available in suitable sizes, all species of crickets are ideal for gecko food.

Where to get them: Gray crickets are now so inexpensive that few hobbyists breed them themselves. If you need only a few, they can be purchased from local pet shops. If you use several hundred to several thousand crickets weekly, purchase them from wholesale producers that advertise in fishing or reptile magazines. You will find the prices quite reasonable when crickets are purchased in multiples of 1,000.

Cricket care: Crickets fed on potatoes are fine for fishing, but you need to offer them a better diet. Feed your crickets a good and varied diet or one of the nutritious, specifically formulated cricket foods now on the market. Fresh carrots, potatoes, broccoli, oranges, squash, sprouts, and chick laying mash, among other foods, will be readily consumed. All offered foods should be sprinkled with calcium-Vitamin D_3, not for the crickets, but for the benefit of the geckos to which the crickets are fed. Crickets can and will be cannibalistic if crowded or underfed. Although crickets will obtain much of the moisture requirements from their fruit and vegetables, they will also appreciate a water source. Crickets will drown easily if they are given just a plain, shallow dish of water. Instead, place cotton balls, a sponge, or even pebbles or aquarium gravel in the water dish. These will give the crickets sufficient purchase to climb back out if they should happen to fall in.

Cricket housing: Keep crumpled newspapers, the center tubes from rolls of paper towels, or other such hiding areas in the cricket's cage. I prefer the paper towel tubes for they can be lifted and the requisite number of crickets shaken from inside them into the cage or a transportation jar. This makes handling the fast moving, agile insects easy. A tightly covered 20-gallon (75.7L) long tank will temporarily house 1,000 crickets. A substrate of sawdust, soil, vermiculite, or other such medium should be present. This must be changed often to prevent excessive odor from the insects.

Breeding your own: If you choose to breed your own crickets, this is not difficult. Keep the cricket cage between 76 and 86°F (24.4–30°C). Place a shallow dish of slightly moistened sand, vermiculite, or even cotton balls on the floor of the cage. The material in this dish will be the laying medium and will need to be kept very slightly moistened throughout the laying, incubation, and hatching process. Adult crickets are easily sexed. Females will have three "tubes" (the central one being the egg-depositing ovipositor) projecting from the rear of their bodies. Males lack the central ovipositor. The ovipositor is inserted into the laying

The gray cricket (Acheta domesticus).

medium and the eggs expelled. The eggs will hatch in from 8 to 20 days, the duration being determined by cricket species and tank temperature. Nutritious food should always be available to the baby cricket.

Uses for the hatchlings: Newly hatched crickets are ideal for tiny geckos. Among the species that will appreciate such minuscule morsels are all sizes of reef and related geckos or hatchlings of many moderately sized species.

Grasshoppers and Locusts

Grasshoppers and locusts (*Locusta* sp. and *Shistocerca* sp. in part) are widely used as reptile foods in European and Asian countries and are commercially available there. In the United States, you'll have to breed them or collect them in the field. This can be done by the deft wielding of a field net. However, grasshoppers are fast, and it may take some time for you to build up your "netting" skills. You may wish to remove the large "hopping" legs before you place these insects in with your geckos.

The grasshopper.

My tip: In some southern areas, large, slow grasshoppers called "lubbers" may be found. Many of these have a brightly colored (often black and yellow or red) nymphal stage that can be fatally toxic if eaten by your geckos. The tan and buff adults seem to be less toxic but their use as a food item is contraindicated.

Waxworms

The waxworm (*Galleria* sp.) is really a caterpillar, the larval stage of the wax moth that frequently infests neglected beehives. These are available commercially from many sources. They are frequently used as fish bait and are available from bait stores. Check the ads in any reptile and amphibian magazine for wholesale distributors. Some pet shops also carry waxworms.

Waxworm tips: If you buy wholesale quantities of waxworms, you will need to feed them. Chick laying mash, wheat germ, honey, and yeast mixed into a syrupy paste will serve adequately as the diet for these insects.

Giant mealworms

Giant mealworms (*Zoophobas* sp.) are the larvae of a South American beetle. They are rather new in the herpetocultural trade and at present (1994), their ready availability is being threatened in the United States by the Department of Agriculture. This is unfortunate, for *Zoophobas* have proven to be of great value to reptile breeders. Although they are still available in many areas of the United States and virtually all over Europe and Asia, it would seem prudent for American herpetoculturists to breed their own.

Keeping your own: *Zoophobas* can be kept in quantity in shallow plastic trays containing 1 inch (2.5 cm) or so of sawdust. They can be fed a diet of chicken starting mash, bran, leafy vegetables, and apples.

Breeding your own: To do this, place one mealworm each in a series of empty film canisters or other similar small containers (to induce pupation) that contain some sawdust, bran, or oats. Nestle the containers together in a larger box, simply to keep them together and so they don't turn over; you don't really need lids because the larvae won't climb out. After a few days the worms will pupate, eventually metamorphosing into a fair-sized black beetle. The beetles can be placed together in a plastic tub, containing a sawdust substrate and some old cracked limbs and twigs, for egg laying (the female beetles deposit their eggs in the crevices in the limbs). The beetles and their larvae can be fed vegetables, fruits, oats, and bran. The mealworms will obtain all of their moisture requirements from the fresh vegetables and fruit.

Multiple colonies: You can keep several colonies rotating to assure that you have all sizes of the larvae to offer your geckos. Although giant mealworms seem more easily digested by the lizards than common mealworms, neither species should be fed in excess.

Mealworms

Long a favorite of neophyte reptile and amphibian keepers, mealworms (*Tenebrio molitor*) contain a great deal of chitin and should actually be fed sparingly. They are easily kept and bred in plastic receptacles containing a 2 to 3-inch (5.1–7.6 cm) layer of bran (available at your local livestock feed store) for food and a potato or apple for their moisture requirements. It takes no special measures to breed these insects.

Film canisters may be used to pupate giant mealworms. The larvae of both types may be housed communally.

Roaches

Although roaches can be bred, it is nearly as easy to collect these as needed. Roaches, of one or more species, are present over much of the world. The size of the roach proffered must be tailored to the size of the geckos being fed. A meal of several small roaches is usually better than a meal consisting of one or two large ones.

Termites

Collect fresh termites as necessary. Should you decide to hold "extras" over, they may be kept in some of the slightly dampened wood in which you originally found them. Termites are most easily collected during the damp weather of spring and summer. One particularly enterprising hobbyist has placed a huge pile of wood shavings some distance from his home, then introduced termites to the pile. From this he can collect these little insects nearly year-round.

Caution: I must mention, that this approach to breeding termites has proven detrimental to the structural integrity of his wood frame house! It is definitely best to collect these insects as needed, then use them immediately.

Fruit Flies

Breeding stock of these tiny dipterids can be purchased from a biological supply house or collected from the wild. Biological supply houses will be able to supply you with flightless "vestigial-winged" fruitflies, a genetic defect that will make handling this insect much easier. Mashed fruit or agar (a seaweed derivative) are good foods. If you use flying species, have flyswatters handy.

Termites.

Houseflies

These may be collected as needed (weather allowing) in commercial fly-traps or bred. Tightly covered, wide-mouthed gallon jars are ideal for this latter purpose. The larvae (maggots) will thrive in putrefying meat, overripe fruit and vegetables, or other such medium. Both larvae and adult flies can be fed to your geckos. The simplest method of introducing the adult flies to the gecko cage is to place the entire opened jar inside the cage. By using this method fewer will escape. The maggots can be removed by hand or with forceps and placed in a shallow dish in the gecko tank.

The housefly.

A young mouse.

Mice

Mice are easily bred. A single male to three or four females in a 10-gallon (37.9L) tank (or a rodent breeding cage) will produce a rather steady supply of babies that can be fed to your larger gecko species. (The colony will also produce a distinct odor, so locate the cages away from your home, in your garage, perhaps.) Leopard, fat-tailed, giant bent-toed, and tokay geckos are just a few of the species that will appreciate and benefit from an occasional baby mouse in their diet.

Use aspen or pine shavings for your bedding. Feed your mice either a "lab-chow" diet that is specifically formulated for them or a healthy mixture of seeds and vegetables. Fresh water must be present at all times.

My tip: *Do not* use cedar bedding for your mice. The phenols contained in cedar can be harmful to your lizards.

Fruit-honey Diet

Two formulas for making the fruit-honey diet are contained in the section on day geckos (page 96). This liquefied, vitamin and mineral-enhanced concoction is a necessity for day geckos and is relished by many other species, as well.

Breeding Geckos

Although many geckos breed well in captivity with little concerted preparation, other species do so only sparingly and then require rather extensive conditioning. Conditioning, as used here, relates to A-1 health, suitable body weight, and reproductive cycling.

Cycling

The term cycling refers to a physiological readying of your gecko for breeding.

Natural rhythms: Under natural conditions, the life cycles of geckos are influenced by seasonal climatic changes. Influencing factors include temperature, rainfall, relative humidity, and photoperiod. The lives of specific gecko species may be affected by some or all of these factors. For instance, seasonal changes in temperature and photoperiod, which are less at the equator than in temperate areas, would influence the activity and lifestyle of equatorial geckos less than it would those of species from temperate areas. Whereas all four seasonal changes would influence temperate-dwelling geckos, only relative humidity and rainfall would figure prominently in the habits of tropical species.

To a lesser degree, these annual seasonal changes can (and if you hope to breed some of the more demanding gecko species, must) be duplicated in the terrarium.

Photoperiod: Photoperiod can be easily duplicated by using a "reversed electric eye" to turn terrarium lights on and off at dawn and dusk. This can also be done manually, or with a simple timer, changing the time settings a little each week (check the weather page in your local newspaper for sunrise and sunset times, and note how these times change as the seasons progress). It may take specimens imported from southern latitudes a season or two to acclimate to the reversed seasons of northern latitude herpetoculturists.

Temperature: Temperature, both daily and seasonal, can be altered with the prudent use of lights and/or heating elements. Temperatures should be allowed to drop slightly on summer nights and slightly more during the shortest days of the year. Some geckos may actually require a month or so of semi-brumation (the reptilian equivalent of hibernation) during the winter months to attain reproductive readiness.

Humidity: Rainfall can be simulated and seasonally altered by expedient misting techniques.

Relative humidity within the cage can be altered by partially or completely covering the terrarium with glass, Plexiglas, or sheet plastic, or by covering or removing plastic covering from outdoor or wire and wood-frame cages.

My tip: For the most part you should strive to have the lowest humidity, the fewest hours of daylight, and the lowest temperatures in midwinter. The greatest amount of all three would be provided in midsummer.

Feeding

Your geckos should be fed most heavily during the long, warm, humid days of summer. As you allow the temperatures to cool, back off a little on food amounts. With warming temperatures, you should again pick up on the amount of food fed to the geckos. Be sure to offer pinkie mice to geckos large enough to eat them. They are one of the better food items available. Gut-loaded crickets, roaches, and mealworms are also ideal. Be sure to provide plenty of calcium and vitamin D_3 throughout the year. These additives are especially important at the time of eggshell formation by adult female geckos and for proper bone development and the growth of hatchlings and juveniles.

Species such as leopard geckos and many of the day geckos are easily bred. Others such as African fat-tails and the various bent-toed species are more difficult. To succeed with many, you may need to experiment with the various cycling factors. With time, as your experiences broaden, you will find yourself making informed decisions and extrapolating from earlier successes. With these experiments will come more successes. Record and share methods, successes, and even failures. All will combine to help you and others with future herpetocultural projects.

My tip: If underweight or in ill health, geckos should not be bred. Egg production and deposition can be very taxing. It can be as difficult to successfully breed obese specimens as underweight ones, although the process is less taxing for overweight geckos than thin ones.

Breeding

What Do You Mean There Are No Males?

Parthenogenesis: Some gecko species can actually reproduce without males. Males are rare in several of the smaller geckos; some populations can actually be unisexual. These are the Indo-Pacific gecko

(*Hemidactylus garnotii*) the mourning gecko (*Lepidodactylus lugubris*) and the stump-toed gecko (*Gehyra ogasawarasimae*). Parthenogenesis may yet be found to occur in other gecko species.

Parthenogenesis involves the production of viable eggs by a female without benefit of male fertilization. The young geckos so produced are always females.

Pseudocourtship: A type of courtship, called pseudocourtship, may be required to stimulate ovulation. On our house walls in southwest Florida, I have watched the introduced and established parthenogenic Indo-Pacific geckos sidle about one another, utilizing movements and motions that, if seen in a bisexual species, could be described only as courtship. Of the several hundred specimens of *H. garnotii* that I have caught and examined, I have never found a male.

Most of the *H. garnotii* in our neighborhood may be seen to be carrying eggs throughout the warmer months of the year.

Although popular hypothesis has it that parthenogenesis is an efficient mode of reproduction, needing only a single specimen to begin a colony, this may not be true. Current scholarly trends of thought are that vertebrate parthenogenesis is not as effective a means of reproduction in the long run as heterosexuality.

Additional studies seem needed.

Reproduction

The vast majority of geckos are oviparous, that is, they reproduce by laying eggs. However, depending on the species, the eggs may have hard, calcareous shells or pliable (and permeable) parchmentlike ones. A very few gecko species are ovoviviparous, producing two living young per clutch.

Live-Bearing (Ovoviviparous) Geckos

Live-bearing in the geckos is restricted to one subfamily, found in the Southern Hemisphere. Geckos of the subfamily Diplodactylinae that bear living young (are ovoviviparous) include:

• All members of the genus *Heteropholis*, New Zealand.
• All members of the genus *Hoplodactylus*, New Zealand.
• Both species of the genus *Naultinus*, New Zealand.
• *Rhacodactylus trachyrhynchos*, New Caledonia.

Egg-laying (Oviparous) Geckos

Hard shells: Two subfamilies in the family Gekkonidae produce hard-shelled eggs. These are Gekkoninae, the typical geckos (usually there are two eggs per clutch) and the subfamily Sphaerodactylinae, the diminutive reef and ashy geckos and allies (usually just one egg per clutch).

Soft shells: All members of the family Eublepharidae, the eyelid geckos, lay soft-shelled eggs. Usually there are two eggs per clutch. Most of the members of the subfamily (Diplodactylinae), of the family Gekkonidae, lay soft-shelled eggs, generally just two per clutch.

Choosing the Deposition Site

Speaking in generalities, there are three types of deposition sites chosen by gravid female geckos and three "kinds" of eggs. The three deposition sites are arboreal, rock-face, and terrestrial, and the three kinds of eggs are hard-shelled adhesive, hard-shelled nonadhesive, and soft-shelled nonadhesive. For the most part, it will be necessary to consider deposition site and egg type together.

Arboreal: Arboreal sites can be used by both egg-gluing and non-egg-gluing gecko species. Captive egg-gluers may place their eggs on terrarium glass or the leaves of stiff-leafed plants; non-gluers will often use the central rosettes of plants such as sansevierias or bromeliads for deposition sites.

Rock faces: Rock faces (including crevices and exfoliations) can be used by either egg-gluing or non-egg-gluing species.

Terrestrial: Both hard-shelled- and soft-shelled-producing gecko species may construct a deposition site in the substrate. They dig directly into the substrate or make a burrow under a rock.

HOW-TO:
Incubation

Incubation techniques are mentioned in the individual species accounts (beginning page 46), as well as elsewhere in the text. Here is an overview.

Removing the eggs:

After your gecko has laid its eggs, remove them as soon as possible if you're planning on incubating them. When you do move the eggs, make sure you do not turn them. Keep the same side upward at all times.

If the eggs are produced by an egg-gluing species, they may be placed in irremovable situations (such as on terrarium glass). In this case it will be necessary to tape a small plastic cup containing a little moistened sphagnum over the eggs, taking care that the moss does not actually come in contact with the eggs. It may be necessary to remoisten the moss periodically. Remember, you are striving for high humidity—*not actual wetness.*

Soft-shelled Eggs

The eggs of the eublepharine and diplodactyline geckos are soft-shelled and permeable. They are capable of desiccation and taking up too much moisture (overhydration). Therefore, incubation conditions need to be fairly precise. Both vermiculite and sphagnum make good incubation media. The vermiculite should be moistened with 4 parts of water to 6 parts of vermiculite, by weight. After it is thoroughly mixed, the eggs

Always keep the same side upward when you move the eggs.

may be placed directly on, or half buried in, the dampened vermiculite. A shallow open dish of water in the incubator will help keep the relative humidity at 100 percent. If sphagnum is used, it should be thoroughly moistened, then squeezed as dry as possible by hand. The eggs can be nestled directly amid the moss. If the moss or vermiculite is too dry or too wet, the eggs will desiccate or overhydrate, respectively. Both conditions can be fatal to the developing embryo. Incubation temperatures that are maintained between 84 to 87°F (28.9–30.6°C) degrees will produce hatchlings of both sexes.

Hard-shelled Eggs

The eggs of rain forest and other high-humidity gecko species will best hatch if kept from directly touching the substrate (sit them atop a small plastic lid or other such support). They will require a 90 to 100% relative humidity to develop properly.

The hard-shelled eggs of many arid-land species will best develop at a 45 to 60 percent relative humidity. Hatching suc-

Tape the bottom half of a paper cup over eggs that are glued to the aquarium wall.

humidity-adapted geckos require a high relative humidity and do best if kept from direct contact with the substrate.

The hard-shelled eggs of many desert and arid-land species develop best at *low* relative humidities.

Sex Determination

The sex of your gecko is determined by the temperature at which the egg is incubated. This is called "temperature dependent sex determination." Cool temperatures produce female geckos; overly warm ones will produce males. Eggs incubated at neutral temperatures produce both male and female hatchlings.

Eggs are placed inside covered containers in the incubator. Use moistened vermiculite or spagnum for the medium.

cess also seems greater with these eggs when they are kept from directly touching the substrate. Again, if the eggs are of an egg-gluing species it may be necessary to adopt special incubation techniques. Attempting to remove the eggs of an egg-gluing species from the area where the female placed them will result in damage to the eggs and death to the embryo inside.

Quick Incubation Guidelines

Be sure to cover the egg containers when they are placed in the incubator.

Soft-shelled eggs: These require a rather precise humidity and substrate moisture.

Hard-shelled eggs: The eggs of rain forest and other

Free-laid eggs can be placed atop a plastic lid and then moved to the incubator.

Geckos of the United States

Of the world's 700-plus species of geckos, only a handful (some 20 or fewer species) occur in the United States. Of these only five—four western desert and one Floridian species—are native; the remaining ones are introduced and established aliens. Geckos are limited in distribution to only the southern tier states, from California in the west to Florida in the east. Even in the comparatively benign climate of these latitudes, most gecko species seek protected areas, and populations of the eastern forms are often the densest amid clusters of buildings, such as dwellings and warehouses.

Two Families

Representatives of two gecko families are found in the United States. The four species of western desert geckos, usually referred to as "banded" geckos, belong to the family Eublepharidae. Pronounced "you-blef-fare-eh-dee," until recently this grouping was considered a subfamily. The members of the Eublepharidae lack the modified subdigital lamellae (toe pads) and have functional eyelids.

The remaining gecko species of the United States are members of the family Gekkonidae (pronounced "geck-on-eh-dee). These are separated into two subfamilies, the Gekkoninae (pronounced as above except for the last

Geckos range in suitable habitats across the southern United States.

Checklist of the Geckos of the United States

Common Name	Scientific Name	Natural Range	Range in United States
Texas banded	*Coleonyx brevis*	USA, Mexico	west TX, south NM
Big Bend	*Coleonyx reticulatus*	USA, Mexico	west TX
Barefoot	*Coleonyx switaki*	USA, Mexico	south CA
San Diego banded	*Coleonyx variegatus abbotti*	USA, Mexico	CA
Tucson Banded	*Coleonyx variegatus bogerti*	USA, Mexico	AZ, NM
Utah banded	*Coleonyx variegatus utahensis*	USA	UT, AZ, NV
Desert banded	*Coleonyx variegatus variegatus*	USA, Mexico	CA, AZ, NV
Asian flat-tailed	*Cosymbotus platyurus*	tropical Asia	FL
Rough-tailed	*Cyrtopodion scabrum*	Africa, Asia	east TX
Tokay	*Gekko gecko*	tropical Asia	south FL
Yellow-headed	*Gonatodes albogularis fuscus*	West Indies Latin America	south FL
Yellow-headed	*Gonatodes albogularis notatus*	West Indies	south FL
House	*Hemidactylus frenatus*	circumtropical	south FL
Indo-Pacific	*Hemidactylus garnotii*	tropical Asia, East Indies	FL, HI
Tropical house	*Hemidactylus mabouia*	Circumtropical	FL
Mediterranean	*Hemidactylus turcicus*	Asia, Africa, southern Europe	isolated colonies in many southeastern states, HI
Peninsula leaf-toed	*Phyllodactylus xanti nocticolus*	USA, Mexico	CA
Fan-toed	*Ptyodactylus hasselquisti*	North Africa, southwest Asia	north FL
Ocellated	*Sphaerodactylus argus argus*	Jamaica, Cuba	south FL
Ashy	*Sphaerodactylus elegans elegans*	Cuba	FL Keys
Reef	*Sphaerodactylus notatus notatus*	USA	south FL

syllable which is "nee"), which includes the "typical" geckos, and the Sphaerodactylinae (pronounced "sfay-row-dack-til-lin-ae"), which are the diminutive reef geckos and their allies.

A great many herpetoculturists specialize in the husbandry of geckos. Some seek out our native and introduced gecko species expressly to collect, keep, and breed; some seek our native and "neo-natives" for photography. This latter pursuit is actually more difficult than the former, for not only are most geckos nocturnal, but even those few of diurnal habits are wary, quick, and elusive.

With few exceptions, this means that photographers must capture and stage their subjects, photograph, then release them. This can be time-consuming, and because most eastern geckos are denizens of urbanized areas, where nocturnal forays (especially when accompanied by flashing strobes) may be viewed with distrust or alarm, successful photographic ventures may take considerable forethought.

Eastern Geckos

To find the geckos of the eastern United States, you will in most cases need to travel to the southernmost tip of the Florida mainland (Palm Beach across to Lee counties, southward) or, in some cases, well down onto the Keys (southern Monroe County).

As of September 1994, 11 species (one with two subspecies) of geckos are known to be more or less securely established in the state of Florida. With a single exception, this being the reef gecko, Florida's gecko fauna is considered to be of introduced status. These are said by researchers to be "introduced and established alien species." They don't belong here. Many biologists don't want them here. But one fact remains—they *are* here! And some of the species are now so widely spread that, barring some climatic disaster, they probably will be here forevermore.

Of our geckos, some can be easily seen and found (various house and reef geckos), others are seen so sporadically (ocellated gecko) that between sightings speculation turns to the possibility of their having been eradicated. About the time it is agreed that this is probably so, another specimen turns up. Where are they in the interim? Who knows? Certainly I don't at present, but I am striving to find out.

Of the geckos now found in Florida, a few are minuscule, a few are of moderate size, and one is a relative giant—and with that said, let's turn to particulars and meet the geckos of Florida, both introduced and native.

Flat-tailed Gecko

The presence of a thriving population of the tiny flat-tailed gecko, (*Cosymbotus* [*Platyurus*] *platyurus*), in a warehouse complex in Pinellas County, Florida was brought to my attention only a few months ago. Since then I have also found the species in two warehouse complexes in Lee County, Florida. *Cosymbotus* was long a mainstay of the pet industry, being imported from southeast Asia as a food species for lizard-eating snakes rather than because of an avid interest in it among herpetoculturists. However, it is a species that is easily maintained in captivity, as long as it is provided with an adequate supply of tiny insects for food.

Cosymbotus is laterally flattened. Its broad tail has serrate edges, and there are skin flanges on the sides of its body and rear legs. When the lateral flanges are spread outward, this little lizard casts little if any shadow; hence, it is nearly invisible against many natural backgrounds. The toes are partially webbed and the digits greatly expanded distally. The pupils are vertically oriented. The flat-tailed gecko is adult at about 3.5 inches (8.9 cm) in overall length.

Cosymbotus is a climbing species that could be termed a "house gecko" for it easily colonizes disturbed areas and is quite common in areas with extensive human populations. Like many geckos, *Cosymbotus* is quite capable of changing its color. These lizards are often lighter at night, at

The tiny Asian flat-tailed gecko, Cosymbotus platyurus, *has only recently become established in Florida.*

The fan-toed gecko, Ptyodactylus puiseuxi, *has long splayed toes with leaf-shaped, terminal subdigital pads.*

times appearing a unicolored, pasty cream. By day, however, they may be quite dark with numerous even darker bands. Male *Cosymbotus* geckos produce a series of clicks as "advertisement" calls or an easily heard, high-pitched squeak if distressed.

Fan-toed Rock Gecko

While attending a conference on the evening of April 9, 1994, researchers Walter Meshaka, Brian Butterfield, and Brian Hauge found several "strange geckos" in a warehouse complex in Gainesville, Florida. The specimens were readily identified as *Ptyodactylus hasselquisti*, a rock-dwelling, North African gecko frequently seen in the pet trade. Commonly known as the fan-footed rock gecko, the agile long-legged creatures were seen well up on the walls of buildings in the company of myriad Mediterranean geckos. Although both sexes were found, no evidence of breeding has yet been noted. Although it would seem premature, based on this single observation, to say that *Ptyodactylus* is currently established in Florida, it is a rather temperature-tolerant species that might be able to withstand the rigors of a north Florida winter. *Ptyodactylus* attains an adult size of nearly 6 inches (15.2°C). The spraddle-legged, spread-toed stance of the long-legged, spindly-tailed *Ptyodactylus* cannot be confused with that of any other gecko species now in Florida.

Fan-toed geckos may be nearly unicolored or rather well-patterned. In keeping with the subdued hues of their natural habitats in the rocky deserts, these geckos are always of pallid coloration. Males produce clicking sounds that are easily audible from a considerable distance.

Tokay Gecko

Not only is the tokay (*Gekko gecko*) the largest gecko in Florida (and one of the largest in the world), it is also the noisiest. Tokays have been found in Lee, Hillsborough, Palm Beach, Broward, Collier, Dade, and Monroe counties. Although often smaller, specimens nearing 1 foot (30.5 cm) in length are frequently encountered.

For years, tokays have been another lizard mainstay of the pet industry. They remain so today. In the erroneous assumption that the big geckos will rid their dwellings of roaches, people have released them in residences and office complexes throughout much of the United States. In southern Florida, where the benign, subtropical climate will allow the species to survive in the wild, tokays have expanded their ranges from the original points of release to neighboring structures. In urban areas, they may now be seen and heard in shade trees and palms, on power poles, and in other such habitats.

Tokays have loud voices. Their two-syllabled calls begin with a chuckle, evolve into a series of "geck-os" or "to-kays," and end in lengthened, slurred notes. These big geckos are primarily nocturnal, but may thermoregulate in sunny areas on mornings following cool nights. Tokays are well able to overpower and consume other lizards, frogs, insects, and other arthropods, but may also accept nestling birds and rodents as well. If threatened with capture, tokays open their mouths widely, "growl" with a drawn out "Gecccck," and, if hard-pressed, will jump toward the offending object and bite. They often retain their grip with a bulldog-like tenacity, tightening up at intervals to convince you that they're still there. Although the consequences of a tokay bite are not serious (hardly more than any other prolonged pinch), it can be a frightening encounter for an unsuspecting person.

These predaceous lizards are too well known by reptile enthusiasts to require much description. They are unmistakably colored, having orange and white markings against a gray or blue-gray ground color. The protuberant eyes may vary from yellow-green to orange. The pupils are complex and vertically elliptical. The toe-pads are large and easily visible. The hard-shelled, paired, adhesive-shelled eggs are deposited in secluded areas of buildings, tree hollows, or other like spots. With her hind feet, the female manipulates the eggs into the spot she has chosen. Wet and pliable when laid, the calcareous, moderately adhesive eggshell soon dries, holding the eggs in the desired spot. Each female may lay several clutches annually. The young exceed 3 inches (7.6 cm) at hatching. Communal nestings occur.

Yellow-headed gecko

In direct contrast to the hulking tokay gecko, the yellow-headed gecko (*Gonatodes albogularis fuscus*) is one of the smallest of species. The yellow-head also differs from most other gecko species by being almost exclusively diurnal in its activity patterns. The yellow-head has round pupils and lacks toe-pads. Very dimorphic, it is only the dark-bodied males (with a bluish sheen, especially at night) that have the yellow (or yellowish) head. A dark shoulder spot, sometimes outlined with blue, is also borne by males. The male's tail may also be yellow and if not regenerated will have a white tip. The females are little grayish lizards that often display a rather pronounced lighter collar.

A native of the West Indies and Latin America, the yellow-headed gecko was introduced in and near Miami and on the Keys. They were once quite common in both areas. However, they now seem uncommon in most of their mainland range and seem increasingly so on the Florida Keys. On a recent photographic venture to the Keys, a two-day search dis-

A male yellow-headed gecko, Gonotodes albogularis fuscus. *This species is a West Indian form now found in Florida.*

closed to me only four yellow-heads—one male and three females. All were sighted in what is for the species a rather typical position—hanging from the underside of low, large-diameter, rough-barked horizontal limbs. These little geckos are extremely wary and difficult to approach.

A second race of yellow-headed gecko (*G. a. notatus*) has recently been found in Broward County,

The female yellow-headed gecko. Note that the coloration is very different than that of the male (above).

Florida. A subspecies indigenous to the West Indies, those present in Florida are of Haitian origin. They are present on land that once belonged to a reptile importer and now is a riding stable. Males of this race of the yellow-headed gecko seem to bear a more prominent blue-outlined black spot on each shoulder than is present on the previously mentioned subspecies, *G. a. fuscus*.

Unlike most other geckos that produce eggs in pairs, the yellow-head lays only a single egg at a time.

House geckos

The geckos with which most Floridians are familiar are the various "house geckos" of the genus *Hemidactylus*. Called "house geckos" because of their fondness for buildings (including houses, warehouse complexes, hospitals, and schools), these little lizards become active at twilight and may gather around lit porch (or other) lights to prey on insects drawn to the glow. There are now four species (two warty and two smooth-scaled) of the genus *Hemidactylus* established in Florida. Two of these, *H. turcicus*, the Mediterranean gecko, and *H. garnotii*, the Indo-Pacific gecko, have now expanded their ranges to other southern states as well. The various *Hemidactylus* species seem to be successfully successful in their efforts at colonization, and where once the Mediterranean reigned supreme, it has now been replaced in many areas by the newer establishees. All of the "hemis" are quite capable of strong color changes. They are darker and (often) more heavily patterned by day, lighter and less contrastingly patterned by night.

Pacific house gecko: It would seem that the most recently found member of this gekkonid quartet is the prolific and aggressive Pacific house gecko (*H. frenatus*). It is a bisexual, mostly smooth-scaled creature that is usually quite light in color. *H. frenatus*

The Indopacific gecko, Hemidactylus garnotii, *is an all-female, parthenogenic species.*

The Mediterranean gecko, Hemidactylus turcicus, *frequents urbanized areas.*

The tropical house gecko, Hemidactylus mabouia, *is another naturalized Floridian.*

does have some rather pronounced spinous scales on its tail.

Indo-Pacific Gecko: *Frenatus* seems still restricted in range to Dade, Monroe, and Lee counties, Florida, but the ease with which it may be confused with the more widely ranging Indo-Pacific gecko may partially account for the paucity of records. *Frenatus* has a white or whitish (sometimes just on the yellowish side of white) belly, whereas the venter of *garnotii* is always of some shade of yellow (often lemon).

H. garnotii is, so far, unique among the geckos in the United States in that it is a parthenogenic (unisexual—all are females) species. Even though unisexual, motions of courtship are indulged in and may, in fact, be necessary to stimulate egg development. Both *H. garnotii* and *H. frenatus* can slightly exceed 5 inches (12.7 cm) in total length.

Although both of these species are called house geckos, they are by no means restricted to such locations. As a matter of fact, all four members of "our" *Hemidactylus* may often be seen on trees and amid debris of both natural and man-made origin.

Mediterranean gecko and tropical house gecko: Of our two warty hemis, the Mediterranean gecko is the more strongly tuberculate (but the tropical house gecko, [*H. mabouia*] has *more* tubercles).

Perhaps the easiest way to distinguish between these two warty species, though, is by noting the shape of the dorsal markings. Those of the tropical house gecko are chevronlike in form, whereas those of the Mediterranean gecko are less precisely defined and never chevron-shaped.

Of our four house gecko species, the tropical (*H. mabouia*) seems the most willing to expand its sphere of activity to tree trunks and debris piles well away from human habitation. Clinging tightly to the trunks, they may

be seen at night in a head-down position. Those that I have encountered in such "natural" settings seem somewhat less wary than when they are encountered on the walls of dwellings.

If you hope to see any of the hemis during a Florida visit, choose a still, humid night on which to look for them. They will be most easily found on the walls of dwellings and warehouse complexes. On breezy or cool nights they often remain near cover. Be keenly observant as you approach the outer perimeters of the halos surrounding lit porch lights or other sources of outdoor illumination. House geckos are often vigilant, and being specifically adapted for discerning movements in the darkness can be alerted to your presence from fair distances. If the geckos have been regularly persecuted by humans, they will be quick to seek cover. The males of all are capable of making weak squeaking sounds. They may vocalize during territorial scuffles or when captured by human or other predator.

Three other geckos occur in the state of Florida. All are in the genus *Sphaerodactylus* and are among the tiniest of gecko species. All lack eyelids and all have expanded terminal digital discs. Of the three, two—the ashy and the ocellated—are introduced, whereas the third—the reef gecko—is Florida's only native gecko species. Like the earlier mentioned yellow-headed gecko, all three *Sphaerodactylus* produce single eggs.

Antillean Ocellated Gecko

The status of the Antillean ocellated gecko (*S. a. argus*) in Florida is fraught with uncertainty. It is unquestionably the most infrequently seen of any gecko species. At present, documented sightings of this 2.25-inch (5.7 cm) sprite in Key West seem to number no more than one or two a decade. Some researchers have tried

The brilliance of hatchling ashy gecko, Sphaerodactylus e. elegans, *dulls with growth to the grays of the adult.*

to explain this scarcity away by posing the question "how much cover does it take to conceal a 2-inch (5.1 cm) long lizard that has long since perfected its skulking techniques?" Well, truthfully, not much. But ashy and reef geckos, neither of which is substantially larger, and both of which are skulkers par excellence, are turned up by the hundreds. It takes no more cover to conceal either of them, but *they* are found. The sighting of an ocellated gecko, however, is truly cause for herpetological jubilation. The ocellated gecko takes its name from the several pairs of dark-edged light nape and shoulder ocelli (which may fuse into striping) that are present on both sexes. The tail is reddish, the body darker. Light lines may be present on the head. The dorsal scales are keeled and a supraocular projection is present above each eye. Although well able to climb, *argus* seems to prefer terrestrial situations where, like other species of this genus, it can take advantage of leaf litter and other ground debris.

Ashy Gecko

The ashy gecko (*S. e. elegans*), a native of Cuba, is the most arboreal of this trio. It is also the largest (by nearly 0.5 inch [1.3 cm]) of the three Floridian species. Considerable ontogenetic color changes occur during the life of this species. Adults are dark with irregular light spots and dots and streaks. Hatchlings are green with dark crossbands and brilliant orange tails. The color change from that of the juvenile to that of the adult is gradual. However, even the darkest of adults is apt to be a pasty white at night. Ashy geckos climb well and often ascend trees, buildings, and other structures in search of insects. On warm, humid summer evenings, I have found ashy geckos to be abundant on the walls of motels and other such structures. They seem less common when house geckos are also present. Although they are reportedly principally crepuscular, those that have been seen in the Florida Keys have been active until long past midnight.

Florida Reef Gecko

The single native gecko, the Florida reef (*S. n. notatus*), is abundant in leaf litter and debris in Dade and Monroe counties, Florida. Reef geckos are particularly abundant (or at least are most easily found) beneath tidal wrack. On some of Florida's lower Keys it is not uncommon to find three or four of these minuscule lizards beneath boards and flotsam just above the high-tide line. Finding them is not the same as capturing them, however. Reef geckos are amazingly fast and adept at instantaneously disappearing into the tiniest of fissures or openings. Reef geckos are also commonly found under debris in the ubiquitous roadside dumping areas so prevalent on the Keys. Principally terrestrial, both sexes of this dimorphic species are darker by day than night. The males are a study of dark on dark—deep brown specks against a slightly lighter ground color. Very old males may be nearly or entirely deep brown. Females are also dark-flecked, but have dark stripes on the head and usually a pair of light ocelli in a dark shoulder spot. The tails of both sexes may be just on the orange side of brown.

To find the sphaerodactyline geckos in Florida, turn debris and leaf litter in suitable areas. Peel the loosened bark shards from both dead and live trees (ashy geckos favor introduced Australian pines), and be ready to grab. These little guys are all alert and fast.

When compared with the brilliance of a day gecko or the uniqueness of a leaf-tailed gecko, the geckos of Florida may not seem very exotic. But the lack of bright color or strange shape does nothing to diminish their appeal for those with broad herpetocultural interests.

Of those discussed, all but the tokay can be colony-maintained in a terrarium as small as 10 gallons (37.9L) in size. I maintained a colony of reef geckos in a 10-gallon (37L) terrarium for nearly a decade and a half. The substrate consisted of about 2 inches (5.1 cm) of clean sand (this was periodically replaced), over which lay a liberal covering of dried leaves. Illumination was provided by an occasional (perhaps once a week) exposure to natural sunlight and the use of an incandescent plant-grow bulb. Room temperature and natural photoperiod prevailed. Although I made no effort to ascertain the individual longevity of the specimens, nearly any time I checked or cleaned I could find two or three adult males, at least that number of females, and numerous juveniles of various sizes. All were fed freshly collected termites and vitamin-dusted pinhead crickets. Because the enclosure was misted daily, all eggs were left in place and, apparently, hatched with no specific incubation procedures. The twin eggs (rarely single) of the various house geckos are every bit as easy to incubate and, because the hatchlings are slightly larger, they are not quite as difficult to raise. Although the eggs of some *Hemidactylus* are moderately adhesive, those of most are deposited on a flat surface such as a windowsill, next to a plant's base in a flowerpot, or beneath debris on the woodland floor. Deposition sites are often used communally and repeatedly. One such site that I recently found on Stock Island in Florida's Keys contained about eight viable eggs and numerous pieces of eggshell from earlier hatchings. The eggs were those of *Hemidactylos mabouia*.

Try your hand with some of these little geckos. If nothing else, success with these will better hone your husbandry techniques, paving your way for greater success with more exotic forms. But along the way, as you work

The color of the Florida reef gecko, Sphaerodactylus n. notatus, *is a study of dark on dark.*

with these Florida species, you may find a true interest developing and that you are trying to justify the costs of a Florida vacation. Don't fight it. It's too late. Succumb graciously. You've been hooked!

Western Geckos

Unlike the geckos of the eastern United States, those of the west may be encountered in urban settings, but they are most common in unpopulated arid-land habitats. Many are best adapted to lives in sparsely vegetated, rocky deserts. Of the six species mentioned here, one, the western banded gecko (*Coleonyx variegatus*), is represented in our west by four subspecies, and another, the Mediterranean gecko, (*Hemidactylus turcicus*), has been discussed in the preceding section on eastern geckos.

Leaf-toed Gecko

The leaf-toed gecko (*Phyllodactylus xanti nocticolus*) is a most "typical"

gecko in external appearances. Having expanded toe-tips and lacking eyelids, the leaf-toe is, except for the earlier-discussed Mediterranean gecko, the only typical gecko of our American west.

The toe-pads consist of two enlarged scales on each toe. This gives these little lizards a "leaf" or "fan-toed" appearance. Leaf-toed geckos attain a 5.5-inch (13.9 cm) overall length.

Leaf-toed geckos are inhabitants of cliff faces, escarpments, and stream-side boulder beds. Rock-surrounded desert springs and arid canyon lands are also favored. In such habitats, leaf-toed geckos seek daytime seclusion in exfoliations, cracks, and crevices from which they emerge under cover of darkness to avidly seek their insect and arachnid prey. Alert and wary, the leaf-toed gecko is an agile and excellent climber. It is quite difficult to approach. The ground color of the leaf-toed gecko usually closely

How to Differentiate the Various United States Subspecies of the Banded Gecko

Subspecies:	San Diego *abbotti*	Tucson *bogerti*	Utah *utahensis*	Desert *variegatus*
Number of pre-anal pores	?	8 or more	?	7 or fewer
Range	southwestern CA; Baja	southeastern AZ; southwestern NM	southern NV; northwestern AZ; southwestern UT	southeastern CA; southern NV; western AZ
Light collar	Yes	Indistinct/ Absent	?	Indistinct/ Absent
Head spotted	No	Yes	?	Yes
Bands with light centers	No	Yes	?	Yes
Dark bands narrower than light	Yes, or of equal width	Yes, or of equal width	No, they are wider	Yes, or of equal width

matches that of the boulders amid and on which it is found. Darker markings, often in the form of irregularly edged crossbands, may be present. Multiple clutches of one or two eggs (usually two) each are laid by adult females. Incubation durations are suspected to be somewhat less than two months. Hatchlings may be found throughout the summer and early autumn months.

The leaf-toed gecko ranges from southern California southward over much of the Baja Peninsula. On the extreme southern Baja it is replaced by the somewhat smaller *P. x. xanti*.

All of the geckos discussed until now in this chapter are members of the family Gekkonidae. All lack eyelids, most have modified scales beneath their toes (toe-pads), and all lay hard-shelled eggs. The remaining four species of geckos, all of the western United States and Mexico,

are somewhat different. All have eyelids, all lack toe-pads, and all lay soft (parchment like) shelled eggs. These four species are members of the gecko family Eublepharidae. All are of similar appearance, varying somewhat in size, markings (which can vary with age), and type of scalation. These are the banded, reticulated, and "barefoot" geckos.

Banded Gecko and Texas Banded Gecko

The most widely ranging of this quartet is the banded gecko (*Coleonyx variegatus*). Occurring in one of several subspecies across much of our southwest and northern Mexico, the banded gecko is the second smallest of our four eublepharine species.

The only other eublepharine gecko with which the banded gecko might be confused is the even smaller Texas banded gecko (*C. brevis*). Without the benefit of knowing the exact point of origin, we find these two species difficult to differentiate. Males are easier to differentiate than females, but even then it will be necessary to have the lizard in your hand. Identification will involve turning the lizard upside down and viewing its venter, in particular its preanal area (the area immediately anterior to the vent or cloaca).

Male eublepharine geckos have a series of enlarged, easily visible pores. Females lack the pores but may have enlarged (even pitted) scales that cross the midventral line in an anteriorly directed chevron. If the lizard at which you are looking is a common banded gecko (*C. variegatus ssp.*), the preanal pores (numbering six to ten in all) will continue uninterruptedly across the ventral midline. The pore forming the apex of the series is situated on the midline. If the lizard at which you are looking is a Texas banded gecko, the preanal pores will usually number fewer than six and those on one side will be separated midventrally from those on the other side by one or more rows of small, unpored scales. In other words, the chevron will be broken centrally.

Besides better-developed preanal pores, male eublepharine geckos have a well-developed spur (visible dorsally) at each side of the tail base.

Banded geckos have finely granular scales. They lack the regularly arranged tuberculate or spinose scales with which the dorsa (backs) of the two largest species, the Big Bend and the barefoot geckos, are studded.

Banded geckos are most commonly seen shortly after dark when they emerge from daytime lairs to forage. At this time they may be seen crossing roadways, often with their tails raised over their backs. If startled they skitter away quickly, their tails writhing like that of an angry cat. The scales on the original tail of a banded gecko are arranged in whorls, and the tail is readily autotomized, either in part, or at the basal constriction. Regeneration is rapid but, even when complete, apparent. The scalation and overall appearance of a regenerated tail is very different from that of the original.

The range of the several races of the common banded gecko extends westward from extreme southwestern New Mexico to southern California and then southward throughout much of western Mexico.

All of the subspecies are quite similar, and again, best differentiated by range.

Because of the high permeability of the shell, female eublepharine geckos must choose their egg deposition sites carefully. It is important that sufficient moisture is present in the substrate to prevent desiccation, but not so much that the embryos drown. In captivity, females will often choose a small container (plastic margarine containers are perfect) holding 1 to 2 inches (2.5–5.1 cm) of slightly moistened sand, vermiculite, or sphagnum moss.

Virtually everything that has been said about the common banded gecko also pertains to the smaller Texas banded gecko. This beautiful little eublepharine is fully adult at about 4 inches (10.2 cm) in length. Males are larger than females. As with the more westerly common banded gecko, Texas banded geckos can display much variation in pattern. The bands are most vividly in contrast and precisely edged on young specimens. With age, some diffusion of pattern is usual. Some old males are quite pale and appear spotted rather than banded.

Big Bend gecko

In 1956, in the Big Bend area of west Texas, a large banded gecko

The preanal pores of the Texas banded gecko (top) are different than those of the common banded gecko (bottom).

Coleonyx variegatus bogerti *is commonly known as the Tucson banded gecko.*

was inadvertently caught in a mousetrap. The catching disclosed a new species, the Big Bend gecko (*Coleonyx reticulatus*), to science. It was not until 1971 that additional specimens were found.

The Texas banded gecko, Coleonyx brevis, *is common and attractive.*

The Big Bend gecko attains an overall length of nearly 7 inches (17.8 cm). Enlarged tubercular scales are interspersed amid the granular scales of the dorsum (back). This large eublepharine is restricted in distribution in the United States to Brewster and Presidio counties, Texas (most of this area is within the Big Bend National Park) but is known in isolated and disjunct areas of northern Mexico as well.

As with the smaller banded geckos, the pattern of the Big Bend gecko is best defined on young specimens. With age an infusion of light pigment invades the dark bands, eventually forming a reticulate, rather than a banded, pattern.

Big Bend geckos have now been determined to be secretive rather than actually rare. Despite being easily automized, their tail is quite prehensile and assists them in retaining their positions as they wander amid their world of rock faces, crevices, and boulders.

As with the other members of the genus, paired eggs are laid at intervals during the warm months of the year.

Barefoot gecko

The single remaining member of this genus to be found in the United States is the barefoot gecko (*Coleonyx switaki*). This large species, to 6.5 inches (16.5cm), barely enters southern California from its Baja stronghold. Throughout its life this is more a spotted than a banded species (but the light spots may coalesce into poorly defined bands). The ground color can be light or dark and usually blends well with the color of the rocks in the gecko's home area.

Dark spinose papillae are interspersed among the granular dorsal scales of this large gecko species. The life history of this gecko has been better studied in Baja than in the United States. Like the Big Bend gecko, the barefoot gecko is probably more secretive than actually rare. It dwells amid rocky rubble, outcrops, and creviced escarpments in arid and semiarid canyon lands and hillsides.

The term "barefoot" comes from the fact that, like other eublepharine species, *C. switaki* lacks any vestiges of the expanded toe-pads that so typify many other geckos.

Captive Care and Breeding

Many American geckos of both native and introduced species can be easily maintained and bred as captives. The methods of inducing breeding are pretty similar, no matter the species involved.

Housing

The terrarium: The size of the terrarium must vary according to the size and number of the species being held captive. For a pair or trio of small species such as the various house, reef, ashy, and yellow-headed, or banded geckos, a 10-gallon (37.9L) terrarium is of adequate size (because of the added height, a 15-gallon (56.8L) "show" tank is even better for the arboreal gecko species).

The substrate: One to 2 inches (2.5–5.1 cm) of fine sand is adequate as a substrate. I prefer to place a covering of several inches of dry leaves atop the sand. Diagonal limbs are places upon which the geckos climb. This enables them to thermoregulate effectively, approaching the tanktop light more closely on cool days. The leaves on the bottom catch and retain droplets of water when the tank is misted, thus allowing a natural drinking method for the little lizards. A potted plant, such as a pothos or philodendron, placed in one corner of the tank will serve a like purpose for those geckos with more arboreal tendencies.

An in-tank temperature of between 74°F (23.3°C) and 88°F (31.1°C)

The Big Bend gecko, Coleonyx reticulatus, remains one of the most poorly known gecko species of the United States.

should suffice. In warm climes, an incandescent tank-top reflector will retain such temperatures. In cooler climes, an under-tank heating pad may need to be used except during the summer months.

If, as I mentioned, you merely allow eggs deposited by your geckos to remain in the substrate, you must remember that a regimen of suitable relative humidity (85 to 100 percent) and incubation temperature (80 to 86°F [26.7–30°C]) must be retained if you expect the eggs to hatch. The humidity can be altered by judiciously misting the cage and substrate. The temperature can be regulated by attaching your heating unit to a thermostat. You may prefer to remove and incubate the eggs where humidity and temperature are more easily regulated. The same parameters as mentioned above should be maintained. Care must be used that the eggs are not turned (rotated) when they are moved. If this is done, the air sac is often disturbed and further development is arrested.

Nutrition

To retain the long-term health of your geckos, it is necessary that they be fed properly. Those that I have kept have fed avidly and lived long lives on a diet of termites, pinhead crickets, and aphids (in season). In Florida, the termites and aphids are easily found throughout much of the year. In more northerly areas, you may have to depend a little more heavily on the crickets and augment these with occasional treats of vestigial-winged fruit flies. These latter are initially available from biological supply houses and are easily raised once acquired.

I believe that providing additional vitamins and minerals for captive geckos is an important consideration. To this end, I dust the baby crickets with a finely powdered supplement that contains both calcium and vitamin D_3. These supplements are provided at least once a week (twice weekly when quickly growing baby geckos are present). Although none of these gecko species are inveterate nectar feeders, I occasionally provide all with a bit of the vitamin-enhanced fruit concoction that I make for my day geckos (see Day Geckos, page 96 for recipes).

The gecko tanks are misted daily, care being taken that at least some of the surface leaves retain pendulous droplets for the geckos to drink.

Reproduction

Inducing breeding may involve nothing more complex than placing both sexes together, or it can be a little more complicated. Even in Florida, ovulation and spermatogenesis by geckos may be controlled by photoperiod (day length), relative humidity, and temperature. Thus, I have found almost all gecko species to breed seasonally, beginning with the lengthening days of spring and progressing into egg laying with the heightened relative humidity created by the advent of late spring and early summer rains. Mimicking these phenomena is rather easily done within the confines of a terrarium. By increasing the hours of illumination and misting the tank a little more frequently and making subtle temperature alterations, you may be able to induce breeding by your geckos at will.

Territoriality (male-to-male sparring and territory protection) is also important in inducing successful breeding. After successfully backing down a subordinate opponent, a dominant male gecko will often dash to a female, indulge in courtship, and breed her.

Although some of the little sphaerodactyline geckos might be termed egg scatterers (merely laying their hard-shelled eggs amid the leaflitter of the woodland floor), others may place their eggs in tree-trunk hollows or in bark crevices, sometimes several feet above the ground. The rather thick-shelled eggs of the sphaerodactylines resist both desiccation and apparently, even if wet directly by rather sustained rains, overhydration.

Other female geckos, among them some of the house geckos, may also merely place their eggs among the leaves, but they seem to choose an area a little more carefully. Frequently their chosen deposition sites are also protected by additional debris or litter. Hollows beneath rocks, cinder blocks, logs, boards, newspapers, or discarded roofing shingles are seemingly favored.

The eggs of some gecko species have adhesive shells and are placed high in hollow trees or near the eaves in buildings where they remain until hatching. One such gecko is the tokay, Florida's largest alien species. Using her hind feet, she works the paired eggs into the area she has chosen. As she places the eggs, their shells are drying. By the time she has accomplished her task, the eggs have adhered and will remain so for the duration. So effective is the adhesion

The tuberculate orange and gray scales of the tokay gecko are quite distinctive.

of the eggs that the hatched shells often remain in place for years, providing evidence of multiple clutching and even communal nesting practices.

Of the Florida geckos, only the tokay is too large to be kept in a 10- or 15-gallon (37.9–56.8L) terrarium arrangement. I would suggest a terrarium of from 29- to 50-gallon (109.8–189.3L) size for a pair of these large aggressive lizards, and a walk-in cage would be even better. I have kept and bred the species in outdoor (southwestern Florida), wire covered, wood-framed cages. The females choose the junction of an upright and the top to deposit their eggs, the incubation of which takes about 54 days. In Florida's hot and humid atmosphere, no additional attention need be given the eggs. In an area with lower humidity, I would tape a cup containing a few spoonfuls of barely moistened sphagnum moss over the eggs (but not touching them). This would raise humidity and help retain an even temperature.

In keeping with their large size, tokays also need larger food items than the other geckos of Florida. Mice, nestling birds, large roaches, adult crickets, grasshoppers, and other similar-sized prey items are all eagerly accepted.

Caution: Tokays are difficult to tame. They can and will bite hard if restrained. Although not serious, the bite can be painful, protracted, and disconcerting. Handle this gecko species with care!

As mentioned earlier, the various eublepharine geckos, the banded, Big Bend, and barefoot, all lay eggs with thin, permeable shells. Gravid females will often enter a container holding a suitably moistened substrate (vermiculite, sphagnum moss, or even clean sand) to lay their eggs. Egg deposition is usually accomplished at night. A proper substrate moisture content is critical to the development of the eggs. Although experience will ultimately prove the best teacher, mixing water and vermiculite (6 parts vermiculite to 4 parts water—by weight, not volume) will provide a suitably moist medium. The eggs are either laid on their side atop this or half buried in a shallow depression. Do not rotate the eggs when moving them. A shallow dish of water is often placed atop the vermiculite to assure a continuous high relative humidity.

The sex of many gecko species of both families is determined by temperature. Low temperatures produce females; high temperatures produce males. The preferred incubation temperature should be between 82 and 88°F (27.8–31.1°C) (see page 64).

Sex of Gecko as Determined by Temperature

Temperature (Fahrenheit)	Sex Produced
below 77°F	High egg mortality. Hatchlings will be females.
78 to 79°F	Females
80 to 83°F	Mostly females
84 to 86°F	Both sexes
87 to 89°F	Mostly males
90 to 91°F	Males
above 92°F	Heightened egg mortality. Hatchlings will be males.

Hemidactylus frenatus, a circumtropical house gecko (see page 52), has only recently been introduced to Florida.

Geckos of Europe

Native European Geckos

Only four species of geckos are native to Europe. All are members of the family Gekkonidae, the "typical" geckos. Of the four, three species have expanded subdigital lamellae (toe-pads) and one does not. None have functional eyelids.

The Mediterranean Gecko

One of the European species, the Mediterranean gecko, (*Hemidactylus turcicus*), also occurs in the United States (see page 52). In Europe, the Mediterranean is often called the " Turkish gecko ." The species may be encountered along the Mediterranean coast. It also occurs in northern Africa and southwestern Asia (and now is found in both North and Central America). Typically bearing dorsal spots that are darker than its base color, some striped specimens have been recorded from Addaya Grande (and surrounding areas), near Minorca.

The toe-pads of the Mediterranean gecko are divided along the midline of the toe. The pads do not reach to the tip of the toes. The claws are prominent and readily visible from all directions.

The Mauritanian Gecko

Tarentola mauritanica is commonly called the the Moorish gecko in Europe and the Mauritanian gecko by the American pet industry. It is of fair length, to 6.5 inches (16.5 cm)—the largest of the European geckos—and typified by a stocky build. Prominent tubercles are arranged in well-separated rows along this gecko's back, sides, and tail. All scales on regener-

ated tails are small. Prominent rounded tubercles are present on the sides of the neck. The coloration of this interesting lizard is of variable earthen tones that usually blend well with its background.

Although a dweller of rocky habitats in areas undisturbed by humans, the Moorish gecko has become a "house gecko" in urbanized areas. In these latter situations it may be seen on walls, roofing tiles, rock and debris piles, and, particularly, on stone walls. It has a clicking call and is quite vocal if restrained. It is principally nocturnal during warm weather, but may be active by day during cool periods.

The toe-pads are prominent and extend to the very tips of the toes. The lamellae are single (undivided) across their entire width. The inconspicuous

Because of its rough scalation, Tarentola mauretanicus *is often called the "crocodile gecko" by pet dealers.*

The European leaf-toed gecko is more readily available in Europe than in the United States.

claws are present only on the third and fourth toes of each foot.

The Moorish gecko is most common in the warmer Mediterranean coastal areas but may be seen in some inland locations. It is also found on the Canary and Ionian Islands, Crete, and north Africa.

The Leaf-toed Gecko

The European leaf-toed gecko (*Phyllodactylus europaeus*) is the smallest of Europe's gecko species. It is also the only one of Europe's four species to lack any enlarged dorsal scales. All scales of this small (to just over 3 inches [7.6] in total length), slightly built species are small and granular. The toe-pads are represented by two enlarged scales on

Kotschy's gecko is one of four European natives.

each toe tip. Like its American counterpart, the European leaf-toed gecko is most common in sparsely vegetated, semiarid rock lands. It also may be found beneath exfoliating bark shards on both fallen and standing trees. It also inhabits stone walls and may occasionally be seen on deserted buildings. Because it usually shuns urban dwellings, this species cannot be considered a "house gecko." Regenerated tails often become swollen and "turnip-shaped."

This nocturnal species is principally an island gecko, occurring on Sardinia, Corsica, islands off of the southeastern French, northwestern Italian, and northern Tunisian coasts and in several isolated populations on the Italian mainland.

Kotschy's Bent-toed Gecko

Cyrtodactylus kotschyi, Kotschy's bent-toed gecko, is the only European gecko species to lack toe-pads. The toes have a characteristic kink, easily visible when viewed from the side. The ground color is similar to the rocks among which this species is usually found. This slender species attains an overall length of about 4 inches (10.2 cm).

Kotschy's gecko alters its activity pattern according to the weather. Often crepuscular and nocturnal during the warm months, it becomes more diurnal when the weather cools. It may occasionally be seen thermoregulating on exposed rocks or walls. Despite lacking toepads, Kotschy's gecko is very agile and quite at home among the rocky habitats it prefers. This species can produce clicking vocalizations.

Kotschy's gecko ranges further inland than the other European members of the family. *C. kotschyi* may be encountered in the Balkans, on Ionian and Aegean Islands, Crimea, and Italy, and well into southwestern Asia.

Captive Care and Breeding

Nutrition

Because all are hardy, the four European gecko species may be easily maintained as captives. Their caging needs are modest and their insectivorous diet fairly easy to obtain, year-round. The size of the food insects must be tailored to the size of the specimen in question. Because of their large size, adult Moorish geckos can easily overpower and consume adult crickets and mealworms. The smaller sizes of the adults of the remaining three species dictates that smaller crickets and smaller mealworms be provided. Sweeping grassy roadside areas with a fine-meshed net during the summer months will often provide you (and your geckos) with a fine array of varied and nutritious insects. Care must be taken, of course, that the insects provided are not from areas where insecticides are used.

Of the European geckos, I have had personal experience only with the Mediterranean and the Moorish. Of the two, the latter is slower and more easily handled.

Housing

Because of their small sizes, pairs of the European geckos can be easily maintained in terrariums of 10 to 15 gallons (37.9–56.8L) capacity. They can be bred by subjecting them to slight winter cooling, by adhering to a "natural" photoperiod, and by taking care that all are healthy and well fed.

Reproduction

Clutches consist of one or two (usually two) hard-shelled eggs that are usually placed beneath or in moisture-retaining debris or rock crevices. The eggs are well able to develop normally with but little moisture exchange. Incubation can vary by species and temperature, but hatching usually occurs in somewhat less than two months. Except for having proportionately larger heads and being somewhat more precisely and brilliantly marked, the hatchlings are miniatures of the adults.

Leaf-tailed and Flying Geckos

Geckos with flattened, leaflike tails can be found both in Australia and Madagascar. Those of Australia, of the genus *Phyllurus*, are only rarely seen in herpetoculture. Among these there are both rock and tree dwellers. Until recently, the geckos of the Madagascan genus *Uroplatus* were seen even less frequently than the Australian forms. But then the island nation of Madagascar began allowing the export of reptiles and amphibians, and leaf-tailed geckos of not just one, but several species became readily available to herpetoculturists. In contrast, the interesting little Asian "flying" geckos of the genus *Ptychozoon*, once mainstays of the pet industry, are now rather infrequently seen.

The southern leaf-tailed gecko is the most common of the Australian forms kept as a captive.

Australian Leaf-tails

The endemic Australian genus *Phyllurus* contains four species. Of these, one has no common name. All are of eastern Australian distribution. Of the four, three—*P. platurus*, *P. cornutus* and *P. salebrosus*—have flattened, leaf like tails with serrate edges. The tail of the fourth species, *P. caudiannulatus*, is heavy at the base, spinose, but rather cylindrical in cross section. This last species is also the only one of the four to lack a prominent lateral fold (or flange). None have prominent toe-pads, but all have slightly swollen, transverse lamellae on the bottom of each "bent," prominently clawed toe.

Southern leaf-tail

Perhaps the best known of these interesting geckos is the saxicolous (rock-dwelling) southern leaf-tail *P. platurus*. It attains an overall length of about 5 inches (12.7 cm), of which slightly less than half is tail length. This amazingly camouflaged species is not uncommon amid the sandstone outcroppings of central coastal New South Wales. I have had several over the years and found them to be hardy and—if not actually grasped—rather trusting little lizards.

The southern leaf-tail is of variable hues that closely match the color of the rocks among which it occurs. Dorsal colors may vary from gray to brown. The limbs are long. Although subdigital lamellae are present, the strongly clawed toes are not noticeably expanded. No preanal pores are present.

Northern leaf-tail

The largest of the genus is the arboreal northern leaf-tailed gecko *P. cornutus*. Individuals with original tails may near (or even slightly exceed) 1 foot (30.5 cm) in length. This tree dweller is noticeably flattened and spinose laterally. The original tail is broad and flattened basally, but has a slender tip. Regenerated tails are flattened and variably shaped, but often look at least vaguely like a violin base in outline.

The northern leaf-tailed gecko occurs in three disjunct and widely separated populations. Two are on the eastern Cape York Peninsula and the third extends in a narrow north-to-south swath from central eastern New South Wales to extreme southern Queensland.

The northern leaf-tail varies from gray to brown, and often has a well-defined reddish vertebral stripe. Vaguely outlined, transverse bandings are often present dorsally.

Rough-throated leaf-tail

North and west of the southernmost population of the northern leaf-tailed gecko in southeastern Queensland, there occurs a newly described look-alike species. This is the (almost) equally large rough-throated leaf-tail gecko (*P. salebrosus*). Whereas the throat scales of cornuta are at most sparsely tuberculate, those of *salebrosus* are highly so. The latter also inhabits a broader range of habitats. Not only does it ascend trees; it dwells amid rocks as well.

Non-conforming member

The 5.5-inch (13.9 cm) long *P. caudiannulatus* is the sole member of this genus without a flattened, leaflike tail. Although heavy, the tail of this arboreal rain forest gecko is nearly round in cross section and tapers to a slender, attenuated tip. This species is found in two disjunct areas of central eastern Queensland. It is an arboreal gecko.

Madagascar Leaf-tails

Among the most unusual of the world's gecko species in appearance are the eight species of Madagascan leaf-tailed geckos. All have well-developed subdigital lamellae and partially webbed toes. Of the eight species, five currently make their appearance in the pet marketplace, but of those five, only two are seen with any degree of regularity. All belong to the endemic gekkonid genus *Uroplatus*. In size and appearance these creatures range from 1-foot (30.5 cm) long bark mimics to 5-inch (12.7 cm) long dead-leaf mimics. All species are magnificent—marvelous, even—but can be quite delicate until acclimated to captive conditions. Some are sea level species that are well adapted to warmth; others are denizens of cool, humid, montane forests and languish

New gecko species are still being found in the wild areas of the world. This is an unidentified leaf-tailed gecko, Uroplatus sp., from Madagascar.

when subjected to temperatures above 70°F (21.1°C).

Virtually all of the Madagascan leaf-tails currently on the market are imports. Many arrive at dealers severely stressed through hunger and crowding and, most especially, suffering from internal parasites and dehydration. In some cases, placing your gecko into a rain and mist chamber may help the lizard reestablish adequate cell hydration.

To be at their most impressive, Madagascan leaf-tailed geckos must have retained their original tails (something that not many specimens do). In appearance, the original tails are gracefully flattened and bear serrate edges. Regenerated tails are never quite as effectively camouflaged, being in both shape and scalation quite different from the originals.

The various Madagascan leaf-tailed geckos are inhabitants of the remaining rain and damp sclerophyll forests of that island country. All are long-legged, lanky lizards that, according to species and preferred habitat, are clad in either the hues and patterns of bark or of dead leaves. All members of the genus are relatively slow moving, depending on their wonderful camouflage rather than speed to avoid predators. Even when thermoregulating (head high to a human and in a head down position) on rather exposed tree trunks, these remarkable creatures are all but invisible.

The giant (or fringed) leaf-tailed gecko

Known scientifically as *Uroplatus fimbriatus*, this impressive, 1-foot (30.5 cm) long gecko is becoming increasingly common in American and European herpetoculture. Skin fringes adorn the sides of the lower jaw, the sides of the body, and the sides of the tail. This is a big brown, brownish gray, or gray lizard that is capable of quite

noticeable changes in color intensity and pattern contrast. The eyes—huge, protuberant, and of a weirdly patterned red on silvery gold color—are the only noticeable breaks in the camouflage of this lizard. By night, these lizards are alert and feed well on large insects; by day, they are quiet to the point of being considered lethargic. This species can tolerate considerable warmth.

Henkel's leaf-tailed gecko

A newly described species, *U. henkeli* is slightly smaller than the giant leaf-tailed gecko. *U. henkeli* is nonetheless an impressive species. The lateral fringes seem less pronounced and *U. henkeli* is capable of assuming an array of colors different from those of *U. fimbriatus*.

Additionally, Henkel's leaf-tail seems somewhat hardier than its larger congener. Despite being new to both taxonomists and herpetoculture, Henkel's leaf-tail is now the species most frequently bred by hobbyists. It seems somewhat hardier than the other species and is able to withstand the rigors of extended transportation better than most of its congeners. Although often of bark gray or brown coloration, some individuals rather regularly assume a spectacular banded pattern of lichen gray on charcoal. This is a warmth-tolerant species.

The mossy leaf-tail

This species owes its common name to the colors and patterns of many specimens. *U. sikorae* ssp. has two subspecies, both less well known than the previous two species. The colors of *sikorae* are those of the ancient trees and fissured rocks—moss green on gray arranged in random lichenate patterns. A species of relatively high altitudes, the mossy leaf-tail prefers somewhat cooler temperatures than either species mentioned earlier— 70 to 75°F (21.1–23.9°C) (with a warmer basking spot) seems ideal. This species has not yet been bred by herpetoculturists.

The lined leaf-tail

Least common of the arboreal *Uroplatus* currently being imported to America, *U. lineatus* is the most atypically marked. Rather than the transverse bars and random lichenate patterns so well displayed by most leaf-tailed geckos, the lined leaf-tail is marked with longitudinal stripes. It is a slender but attractive species about which herpetoculturists know little. It is imported so rarely that the prices remain artificially high. If, like the other species of this genus, color is indicative of preferred habitats, the terracotta to light red-brown ground color of the lined leaf-tailed gecko would suggest it to be an inhabitant of areas predominated by red clay, red rock and red-barked trees.

The phantastic leaf-tail

U. phantasticus is a most remarkable species amid an equally remarkable genus. This little dead-leaf mimic of the higher altitudes (hence cooler temperatures) is sexually dimorphic and of variable coloration. Its demonic expression with its pointed eyelids may be viewed against a ground color that ranges from pale lavender to earthen brown. Attaining only 4 to 5 inches (10.2–12.7 cm) in length, this is not only one of the less frequently seen species, but is one of the most sought after and expensive as well. When kept cool, the phantastic leaf-tailed gecko seems to be rather hardy, eagerly accepting small crickets and waxworms. Like other leaf-tails, imported specimens of this wonderfully attractive gecko species often lack their tails entirely or have tails in the initial stages of regeneration. Although this certainly detracts somewhat from their appearance, hobbyists and zoos continue to snap up all specimens offered.

This species has now been captive bred.

Of the remaining Uroplatus species–*U. ebenaui, U. alluaudi,* and *U. guentheri*—only the first is now in herpetoculture.

Captive Care and Breeding

Housing and Nutrition

There are several essentials that must be accomplished if you wish to succeed with these interesting and increasingly frequently seen lizards. Firstly, the proper temperature must be selected and maintained. Secondly, humid (but not wet) caging must be provided. Thirdly, healthy stock must initially be procured. Fourthly, adequate water and an ample and varied diet must be given the lizards.

Reproduction

Of the leaf-tails, only the giant fringed, phantastic, and Henkel's have been captive-bred. Leaf-tailed geckos are easily sexed. Adult males have a decidedly swollen hemipenial area.

Despite the persistently arboreal tendencies of many of these geckos, all seem to lay their eggs in the substrate of their cages (or forest floor). The eggs, numbering two per clutch, are nonadhesive and take somewhat less than three months to hatch. Like the adults, the hatchlings are rather slow moving, apparently relying on their marvelous camouflage to avoid detection.

Two baby *U. henkeli* that I hatched here began accepting "fly-sized" crickets and houseflies only a day or two after hatching. They grew quickly and within six weeks had graduated to half grown crickets and waxworms. To provide them with ample calcium and the ability to properly metabolize it during this very important stage of their lives, the food insects were dusted with additives twice weekly.

Some Henkel's leaf tailed geckos, Uroplatus henkeli, *are handsomely marked while others are less so.*

The mossy flat-tailed gecko, Uroplatus sikorae ssp., *appears to be covered with lichens.*

Uroplatus lineatus, *the lined leaf-tailed gecko, is the only of the leaf-tails with distinctive striping.*

Uroplatus phantasticus, *the "phantastic" leaf-tailed gecko, is a most remarkable appearing and seldom seen lizard.*

Following the nightly cage misting, hatchlings would lap pendulous drops of water.

Although the keeping of these geckos is best reserved for experienced hobbyists, there can be no denying that they are uniquely interesting creatures, well worth all efforts.

Flying Geckos

The first among those species rather well known to advanced hobbyists worldwide are the little bark-colored "flying geckos," of the genus *Ptychozoon*. A series of dark, wavy dorsal markings is usually visible. Like most geckos, flying geckos can change their color somewhat. Merely variations of a theme, the ground color can lighten or darken, and transverse markings may fade from a strong contrast to near invisibility.

These are wonderful little arboreal geckos with large heads, flattened bodies, lateral skin folds on body and limbs, webbed toes and scalloped edges on their flattened tails. Although they are utterly incapable of flight, the lateral skin flanges when extended do create a greater surface area that allows the geckos to parachute for fair distances. When sitting quietly, typically in a head-down position on a tree trunk, these little lizards are virtually invisible. At times, these geckos may even hang inverted on the underside of horizontal limbs. Even when captive and known to be within the confines of a terrarium, flying geckos can be amazingly difficult to find.

There may be as many as five species of flying geckos, all amazingly similar in appearance. Of the five, two species appear rather regularly in the American and European pet trade. These two are *P. lionatum,* which lacks enlarged scales on the dorsum, and *P. kuhlii,* which has enlarged tuberculate scales interspersed among the normal granular dorsal scales.

Most of the specimens available are wild-collected imports.

Lion-tailed flying gecko

P. lionatum is a little baggy-appearing gecko that may attain an overall length of about 6 inches (15.2 cm). Of this, about half is tail. The sides of original tails are scalloped anteriorly but smooth-sided distally.

Lion-tailed flying geckos are inhabitants of the forested areas of Burma and Thailand. They seem to tolerate the presence of people well and are becoming "house geckos" in some parts of their range.

Female flying geckos return to chosen deposition sites time and again. The area chosen may be a tree hollow, behind exfoliating bark or rocks, or other such secluded area. Captive females may even choose a corner angle of their terrarium as a support, gluing the eggs to the glass. The paired eggs have adhesive shells. Using her hind feet, the female carefully works the eggs into place while the shells are damp and pliable. As the shells dry and solidify, the eggs adhere tightly to their support. At a temperature between 80 and 85°F. the eggs will hatch in about ten weeks. The hatchlings are nearly 2 inches (5.1 cm) in overall length.

A newly hatched Henkel's leaf-tailed gecko rests quietly above the egg from which it emerged. A second egg is about to hatch.

Popular Terrestrial Geckos

The Leopard and Fat-Tailed Geckos

Without question, the gecko species most favored by herpetoculturists is the hardy and attractive leopard gecko (*Eublepharis macularius*). Once familiar with the leopard gecko and its wiles and ways, many hobbyists branch out to a species of similar morphology but very different habits—the fat-tailed gecko (*Hemitheconyx caudicinctus*). This second species remains a very distant runner-up but is gaining new fans with each passing day.

Although many times I have found it difficult to justify my seemingly incompatible position of both conservationist *and* pet ownership advocate, such is not the case when I discuss either or both of these eublepharine gecko species. The reason I do not find these two problematic is simple: captive colonies now produce sufficient numbers of leopard geckos to virtually sustain the demand of hobbyists, and the increasing number of captive-bred fat-tails is quickly closing the gap between the demand and the supply for this species as well. Thus, despite the fact that thousands of these lizards are sold annually, relatively few wild-caught specimens are imported. There is minimal drain on wild populations.

That captive-breeding programs are able to supply the demand for these increasingly popular lizards speaks well for not only the hardiness and adaptability of the leopard and fat-tailed geckos, but for the knowledge and diligence of that rather new breed of reptile enthusiast, the herpetoculturist. Indeed, it is largely due to the promotional efforts of these latter (be they large and on the commercial level, or individual hobbyists) that leopard and fat-tailed geckos have attained the immense popularity that they now enjoy in the reptile-keeping hobby.

Family Characteristics

Leopard and fat-tailed geckos are two of the larger species of the gecko family Eublepharidae. This is a primitive subfamily containing terrestrial members that share such characteristics as having well-developed, fully functional eyelids and that lack the toe-pads so typical of many of the geckos in the family Gekkonidae. Additionally, all eublepharine geckos produce soft, rather than hard-shelled, eggs and are more or less restricted to desert and dry savanna habitats.

Relatives of the leopard and fat-tailed geckos occur in suitable habitats in both North and Central America, Japan, southeast Asia, and eastern Africa. Probably the most primitive member is *Aeluroscalabotes felinus*, the cat gecko of southeast Asia. Many of the eublepharines have the caudal (tail) scales arranged in prominent whorls, and the tails of all are very easily broken. Although they regrow quickly, the regenerated tails differ from the originals in both shape and color. Most often the regenerated tails of the leopard and fat-tailed geckos are turnip-shaped or bulbous in configuration, bear an irregular scalation, and are of a paler color.

The natural history of the leopard gecko is much better known than that of the fat-tail. Both, however, are long-lived (15 to 22 years not being uncommon), large-headed, heavy-bodied lizards that are more precisely patterned and brilliantly colored when young. Leopard geckos are clad in yellows and grays, fat-tails in browns and tans. With increasing age, the striking banded pattern of the baby leopard gecko breaks into a pattern of spots and reticulations. Adult fat-tailed geckos retain the strongly banded pattern of babyhood. A rather uncommon color phase of the fat-tailed gecko has a broad white middorsal stripe on both head and body. Both tame reasonably well and seem to wear perpetually bemused smiles.

Housing

Because neither leopard nor fat-tailed geckos are overly active, their terrariums can be relatively small. A terrarium made from a 10-gallon (37.9 L) tank is sufficiently large for one male and three females. It should be remembered that fat-tailed geckos are capable of withstanding *slightly* more humid conditions than those preferred by leopard geckos. In fact, a slightly higher relative humidity may even be beneficial to the former.

The substrate for both species may consist of 1 to 2 inches (2.5–5.1 cm) of sand, small pebbles, cypress mulch, or other such material. The use of sharp-edged silica aquarium gravel is contraindicated, for intestinal impaction may occur if the lizard accidentally ingests any substantial amount while feeding. Several cork bark or similar hiding places should be provided for these nocturnal lizards. A low receptacle of clean water should always be present.

Diet

By nature, eublepharine geckos feed upon living insects and other arthropods. For captives, crickets, common and giant mealworms, wax-worms, butterworms, and other such commonly available insects are all excellent food items. Newly born (pinkie) mice are also eagerly accepted by many, if not most, larger gecko specimens. A varied diet is better than a constant one, and the size of the food items must be tailored to the size of your lizards. If neither yard nor garden insecticides are used, an even more variable diet can be offered your lizards. Not only are such things as sow bugs and hairless caterpillars relished by geckos, but wild insects generally contain more nutrition than domestically raised ones. If store-purchased insects are the exclusive food of your lizards, be certain to dust the insects liberally with a calcium and vitamin D_3 supplement. This is especially important during periods of rapid growth or egg production, when juveniles and females, respectively, will require larger than normal amounts of calcium for healthy bone formation and eggshell production.

Prey acquisition: The hunting strategy of eublepharine geckos is both interesting and, at times, comical. The approach by the lizard to a food item may be either stealthy or darting, and is often accompanied by an accentuated amount of tail-writhing and posturing. The final grasping of the food item is rapid and sure. Mastication is thorough. The strategy used may be as individual as the lizards themselves.

Reproduction

Sexing: Most of the leopard and fat-tailed geckos offered by the pet trade are of juvenile to subadult size. (Of these two species, the leopard gecko seems to grow slightly the faster, often

The African fat-tailed gecko, Hemitheconyx caudicinctus, *is the second most popular of the eyelid geckos.*

This is a somewhat unusually patterned leopard gecko, Eublepharis macularius.

attaining sexual maturity in slightly less than a year.) Adults may be easily sexed by comparing the areas immediately anterior and posterior to the cloacal opening (anus). To do so, it will be necessary to grasp your lizard (firmly yet gently) and turn it upside down. It will be seen that males, especially those that are sexually active, have a vaguely chevron-shaped (apex anterior) series of enlarged preanal pores as well as a proportionately bulbous tail base. The bulbosity is formed by the hemipenes. These characteristics are lacking on females.

Interestingly (as with many lizards), sex is determined by incubation temperature, rather than genetically. Ideally, incubation should be accomplished at a temperature of from 84 to 86°F (28.9–30°C). Within this rather narrow temperature range, both sexes will be produced. If cooler, the sex ratio of the hatchlings will be skewed in favor of females, and if warmer, a preponderance of males will occur (see chart, page 64).

Adult behavior: Male eublepharine geckos are highly territorial. No more than a single male may be kept to each cage, but usually several females may be kept with him. Occasionally even the females can be aggressive, and until your colony is established it will be necessary to monitor the activities of all. If severely subordinate, a lizard may refuse food and soon succumb.

Breeding: Although the breeding season for your geckos may vary slightly according to your latitude, it usually encompasses a seven- or eight-month period that begins in late autumn or early winter. Although I always preconditioned my breeders by "cooling" them to room temperature (in Florida, 70°F [21.1°C] days and 60°F [15.6°C] nights) for the month of October, many breeders claim this to be unnecessary. Except for October,

I kept a heat tape activated beneath one end of the gecko's terrariums both day and night. I also utilized a "natural photoperiod" throughout the year and believe this to be beneficial. When reconnecting the heat tape in early November, I also increased the amount of food offered the geckos, allowing them to feed until sated. (Thin lizards will produce fewer, weaker, eggs.) An egg-deposition area, such as a low 2-inch (5.1 cm) margarine cup containing barely moistened sand or vermiculite, was nestled into the sand near one corner. Seldom would the female fail to use this. The eggs were removed on the morning following deposition and placed in a temperature-controlled Styrofoam incubator.

Incubation: A healthy female eublepharine gecko should produce several clutches of two eggs each over the breeding season. Incubation duration varies with temperature (shorter when warmer), but will probably average about 55 days. A number of incubation media are successfully used. Among others are sphagnum, peat, sand, perlite, and vermiculite. The eggs of eublepharine geckos are soft-shelled, hence moisture-permeable. The amount of moisture contained in the incubation medium is critical to the development of the eggs. Either too much or too little moisture will cause egg death. The moisture content of all media must be just sufficient to keep the eggs turgid, allowing neither the desiccation nor overabsorption that will cause the death of the embryo. Experience will truly be your best teacher for determining your incubation techniques. In the interim, a mixture of 6 parts vermiculite to 4 parts of water (by weight) will probably suffice. Most breeders also place a shallow dish of water atop the vermiculite to assure a relative humidity close to 100 percent is constantly maintained. The eggs may be laid on their sides atop the vermiculite or be buried about half way in a shallow depression. Extreme care should be used that the eggs are not rotated on their longitudinal axes when they are being moved.

Because they are hardy and easily cared for, both leopard and fat-tailed geckos are ideal lizards for beginners. The fact that they are attractive and prolific adds an extra dimension of enjoyment to their maintenance. Try a pair (or more). I doubt you will be disappointed.

Other Terrestrial Geckos

Besides leopard and fat-tailed geckos, there are several additional terrestrial geckos that are rather frequently seen in the pet trade. Among these are the frog-eyed geckos, the Namibian sand gecko, the helmeted gecko, the web-footed sand gecko, and the ocelot gecko.

The Frog-eyed Gecko

Of the several frog-eyed geckos, it is the greater (*Teratoscincus scincus scincus*), that is the most frequently offered. This robust species is adult at between 4.5 and 6.25 inches (11.4–15.9 cm) in total length. The several species of frog-eyed geckos share a reputation of being difficult captives. In fact, they are relatively hardy if a terrarium habitat is constructed that meets their rather specific requirements.

A wide-ranging species, the greater frog-eyed gecko can be encountered in desert and other arid-land habitats from southern Asia (including southern areas of the former U.S.S.R.) to western China and many mid-eastern countries, and on to Pakistan. This species is an excellent digger, excavating its burrows down through the dry surface sands well into the moister subsurface sands. The desert areas in which this Asian gecko dwells are subject to decided day and night, as well as seasonal, temperature changes. These temperature extremes should be considered when housing the species as captives.

These vocal geckos are crepuscular and nocturnal as well as seasonal in their activity patterns. Winter cold can bring about rather extended periods of brumation. They are, however, active throughout the warmer seasons of the year. Their sharp call notes denote both territoriality and anger (the two not being awfully distantly removed). But unlike other geckos, frog-eyes have a secondary method of producing sounds. When the tail is writhed, as it is when the greater frog-eyed gecko becomes defensive (or otherwise excited), a scraping sound is produced. This is caused by the large supracaudal scales (the scales on the top of the tail) rubbing together.

Frog-eyed geckos are clad in scales of earthen hues. The dorsal background coloration may be yellowish or buff. Against this are darker and lighter spots or broken stripes. The sides are pale and the venter is immaculate white. The scales of the head are small. Those of the trunk (including venter), limbs and tail are noticeably enlarged and "fishlike" (cycloid), with the scales along the top of the tail being the very largest. The head of this gecko species is broad but somewhat foreshortened. The eyes are prominently large and rimmed with scales that serve as eyelashes. The limbs are long and powerfully built. Rather than expanded climbing lamellae, the geckos of this genus have a fringe of comblike scales along their toes. These scales permit greater ease of motion in fine-sand habitats. This gecko is also an accomplished burrower.

The skin of all species of frog-eyed geckos is very delicate and permeable. It can be easily torn if the gecko squirms while being handled. The tail is remarkably easily autotomized, at times being broken with what seems merely a touch. If your gecko is healthy, the skin will heal and the tail will regenerate. However, both problems (and especially the first) are stressful for the animal. I suggest that the members of this genus be "cupped" (directed into a jar or glass) so that they can be moved without actually being restrained in the hand.

The very thin skin of the members of the genus *Teratoscincus* does little to inhibit desiccation. The thin integument is extensively vascularized, readily allowing gas and moisture exchange. It is for this reason that these geckos burrow through the dry surface layers of sand and terminate their burrows in the moister subsurface areas. If their terrarium is set up in a like manner, *Teratoscincus* will thrive. To even come close to accomplishing this will require several inches of sand substrate. I suggest a minimum of 8 inches (20.3 cm), with from 12 to 14 inches (30.5–35.6 cm) being much better. To moisten the bottom layers of sand without saturating the top ones will require the insertion of a small-diameter standpipe or some rocks on one end of the terrarium that reach from the bottom to above the level of the top of the sand. A small amount of water poured into the pipe or in the fissures in the rocks will flow directly into the bottom layers of sand without wetting the top. If an earthen (clay) pipe of suitable diameter is used, it can serve dual purposes. Tilted so that it provides easy ingress and egress, besides serving as a water conduit, it provides the geckos a daytime hiding area.

The weight of the sand in a frog-eyed gecko terrarium can be considerable. Care should be given that the terrarium has been placed in its permanent location before the sand is added and dampened, and that the stand on which the terrarium is placed is sturdy enough to hold the weight.

A pair of frog-eyed sand geckos can be housed in a terrarium having a floor space of about 12 × 30 inches (30.5 × 76.2 cm). Daytime temperatures of 84 to 94°F (28.9–34.4°C) localized areas—not the entire terrarium—can reach slightly higher temperatures for short periods of time are best. The deep sand substrate can be warmed from beneath by the prudent use of heat tapes and heating pads and from above by heat lamps. It is important that a thermal gradient be provided, with the sand at one end of the tank being cooler than that at the other. This will allow your geckos to choose the sand temperature at which they feel most comfortable. The entire terrarium should be allowed to cool by 10 to 15°F (5.6–8.4°C) at night.

During the warm months of summer, frog-eyed geckos should be fed often. They should be fat and healthy prior to the winter cooling that is to follow. The winter cooling period should last from five to eight weeks. During that period daytime highs of 60 to 65°F (15.6–18.3°C) and nighttime lows of 50 to 60°F (10–15.6°C) will suffice. This will condition the lizards for breeding. It is likely that the lizards will become entirely inactive and remain in their burrows during this cooling period. Food will be unnecessary during this period. It is because of this fasting that it is so necessary that your geckos be in excellent health and have good body weight prior to cooling. Care must be taken that the sand substrate not be allowed to dry out during this period of semi-brumation. Also keep a surface water dish available and filled at all times.

The diet of this gecko in the wild consists largely of beetles. Captives will eat mealworms and their beetles, giant mealworms and their beetles, crickets, grasshoppers (not lubbers, which are variably toxic), and other non-noxious beetles. Some specimens will also accept newly born mice. Frog-eyed geckos can be cannibalistic, consuming lizards of other species as well as their own hatchlings.

Properly conditioned female frog-eyed geckos will deposit several clutches of two (rarely one) hard-shelled but very easily damaged eggs during the summer months. Quite unlike the eggs of most other gecko species that require a high humidity, the eggs of the frog-eyed sand geckos do not. Preferred humidity is in the 40 to 55 percent range. At 80 to 90°F (26.7–32.2°C), the incubation period will be from 70 to 100 days. The moisture content and humidity in the incubation medium that would be "normal" for other species can prove fatal to the developing embryos of *Teratoscincus*. This species is not yet being captive-bred in large numbers. Most of the specimens currently being offered in the pet trade are wild-caught imports.

Because of their easily torn skin, greater frog-eyed geckos, Teratoscincus scincus *ssp. should not be handled.*

Hatchlings of this species are much more brilliantly colored than the adults, being a rather bright yellow with black crossbands.

Collectively, frog-eyed geckos are among the more aggressive (defensive?) gecko species. Their defense posture is stylized and interesting. When approached by a predator (or your hand) the frog-eyed gecko assumes a tiptoe stance, mouth open, throat (gular) area expanded, back humped and tail writhing. If the threat continues the gecko will squeak, dart toward the object, deliver a slicing bite, then turn and dart to its burrow, into which it will dash headlong if allowed.

Although they may be somewhat more demanding than many geckos in their terrarium needs, frog-eyed sand geckos are very interesting and well worth the extra effort required. You will need to heed the handling cautions delineated earlier in this account. The probability of your specimens sustaining torn skin and tail loss during what you might consider a "routine" procedure must always be a very real concern.

Not all of the members of the genus *Teratoscincus* have enlarged "fishlike" scales. The somewhat smaller species, *T. microlepis*, often called the "lesser frog-eyed gecko" is clad in small granular scales. This very attractive lizard may be successfully maintained in the manner just discussed.

The Web-footed Sand Gecko

The web-footed sand gecko (*Palmatogecko rangei*) is a specialized, "sand swimmer" endemic to the fog-shrouded Namib Desert to southwestern Africa. There, it dwells among the ever-changing dunes of this strangely complex and unique habitat. Besides being of slender build, the web-footed gecko is a small gecko species, attaining only a 4-inch (10.2 cm) overall length.

Palmatogecko is a persistently nocturnal species that is active throughout the year when climatic conditions are suitable.

Males produce clicks and squeaks, both during territorial displays and when restrained.

The web-footed gecko is clad in finely granular scales similar in color to those of the sands on which it dwells. Tans, buffs, and the palest of grays are the usual hues. The two most unusual external characteristics are the feet and the eyes of this species. The toes are webbed to their tips with a thin pliable skin. This gives the lizard the appearance of having snowshoes. The eyes are very large and protuberant. The iris of each is colored in dark and red pigments that are especially apparent in well-lit situations when the vertical pupils are tightly contracted.

The coastal Namibian desert is one of the world's most unusual habitats. Because of the proximity of cold austral ocean currents to the coast, this desert is often shrouded in dense fogs. It is also different from most deserts in that it has minimal daytime and nighttime temperature differences. This, then, is the home of *Palmatogecko rangei*, and it is these conditions that you must strive to duplicate if you hope to keep the web-footed gecko successfully in the terrarium.

As a result of the persistent fogs in this desert habitat, some moisture often exists beneath the surface of the sands. It is within this layer of slight moisture that the geckos construct their home burrows. This is not a habitat easily duplicated in the home terrarium, but is the one for which you are striving. See the captive-care suggestions for the frog-eyed gecko, page 78, for terrarium setup procedures. A few flat rocks (such as pieces of shale) and drought-tolerant plants (sansevierias or haworthias) can be provided for cage furniture. Pieces of cork bark and the bleached, hollowed skeletons of opuntia (cholla) cactus can also be supplied but are not absolutely necessary. It should be remembered that, although web-footed geckos are desert dwellers, they construct rather deep burrows to escape the worst of the heat. In the terrarium daytime temperatures of between 88 to 95°F (31.1–35°C) on the sand surface are suitable. The below-surface temperature should be somewhat cooler. Nighttime temperatures should be allowed to drop by only a few degrees, if at all. Web-footed geckos will drink water from flat receptacles, but also will lap the droplets from the rocks in their terrarium if these are misted during the gecko's period of activity. Web-footed geckos prefer prey insects of small size and are especially fond of termites and baby crickets.

Web-footed geckos have a reputation of being delicate captives. Although it is true that they prefer rather exact terrarium conditions, when

The web-footed gecko, Palmatogecko rangei, *is a specialized dweller of the fog deserts of southwestern Africa.*

these conditions are met, and when adequately small food insects are provided in sufficient quantity, I have found the species to be quite hardy. As with all geckos, to prevent aggression, no more than a single male should be kept in each terrarium. From one to several females may be housed with each male. Successful captive breedings of the web-footed sand gecko have recently been reported.

The Helmeted Gecko

The helmeted gecko (*Geckonia chazaliae*) has only recently become available to American herpetoculture. Although only 3.5 inches (8.9 cm) in length when adult, it is big-headed and robust.

The arid-land dwelling helmeted gecko hails from North Africa. It seems to prefer rocky and gravelly areas.

Weather permitting, *Geckonia* is active year-round. It is capable of brumating for short periods if necessary. Both crepuscular and nocturnal in nature, captives may also forage by day, especially when in reduced-light situations.

The vocalizations of the helmeted gecko are low-pitched clicks with little carrying power.

This desert and dry savanna gecko is clad in earthen-colored scales. The background color can vary from reddish buff to pale gray. Dark and/or light markings may or may not be present. The scalation is irregular and variably tuberculate. The common name is derived from the row of large conical scales at the rear of the head. The head is proportionately large and the large, heavily browed eyes are lidless. The legs are sturdy, the toes short, flattened, serrate laterally, and webbed basally.

Geckonia is an interesting and normally slow moving little lizard. When startled it may move in short bursts of speed. A trio that I kept for a few years thrived in a 15-gallon (56.8 L) capacity terrarium. The substrate was a couple of inches of sand over which was strewn an ample scattering of pea- to penny-sized chipped rocks. When still, the little geckos with their variable color and variably sized and roughened scales were nearly invisible against this background. This gecko species is quite hardy and undemanding. Heat tapes provided daytime temperatures of 85 to 96°F (29.4°–35.6°C). The tapes were turned off in the evening, allowing nighttime temperatures to drop into the 70sF (20sC). For one month during the winter, temperatures were dropped by an additional 10°F (5.6°C). Helmeted geckos drink readily from a low water dish when thirsty but really seem to need little moisture. Those I have had have preferred slow crawling prey to fast moving crickets, but after a time would readily eat nearly any insects offered. They were fed sparingly during the month-long period of winter cooling. Helmeted geckos are being bred both in the United States and in Europe on a regular but sparing basis. At 86°F (30°C), the eggs hatch in about 70 days. The only female I have had that produced eggs delivered three clutches at about 23-day intervals. One egg from each clutch was infertile.

"Cute"—a word not regularly applied to reptiles—is the term often applied to these unique little lizards. The availability of *Geckonia* varies month by month and year by year. At some times they are so readily available that the prices drop to near $50 each. At other times, helmeted geckos may command three times that much or not be available at all. Although I consider this species rather easily kept, it displays just enough idiosyncrasies to be challenging. Therefore, I suggest that helmeted geckos are best suited for experienced hobbyists.

The Namibian Sand Gecko

The Namibian sand gecko (*Chondrodactylus a. angulifer*) has long been a favorite of herpetoculturists.

This robust and pretty gecko species attains an overall length of about 6 inches (15.2 cm). Of this length, less than half is tail length. It is native to southern and southwest Africa where it dwells in deserts and savannas.

The basically nocturnal Namibian sand gecko is active during the warmer months of the year. It may become less so during the austral winter. Captive specimens reproduce better when cooled somewhat during the short days and long nights of winter. Actual brumation does not seem to be necessary either for the well-being of the lizards or to assure fertility.

Male sand geckos are capable of producing clicking vocalizations. These are most frequently heard during territoriality disputes or when the gecko is restrained.

Sand geckos are sexually dimorphic. The males are somewhat the larger of the sexes and bear from one to several pairs of dark bordered white ocelli along their back. The females lack the ocelli, having instead several posteriorly directed dark chevrons on their backs. The tail of the female is more prominently banded than that of the male. The overall color scheme varies from reddish buff, blending quite well with the sands on which these lizards dwell. The head of both male and female are large and a fringe of serrate scales is found beneath the toes. These latter lead to a second common name, this being the "comb-toed sand gecko." The large eyes lack functional lids but are partially shaded and protected by a flange of enlarged scales.

It would appear that the noticeably short toes of this gecko species are not well adapted for digging. Thus, although in the wild *Chondrodactylus* are often found in burrows during the day, more often than not they seek out vacated burrows of other desert animals. In the terrarium they readily accept rock caves or other such areas of seclusion. This gecko species habitually "stands tall" at the mouth of its burrow, its legs nearly fully straightened. It seems alert and is ever ready to retreat back into the burrow if danger threatens. *Chondrodactylus* is, itself, a fearsome predator, easily overcoming insects, arachnids, and even smaller lizards. As captives, most adults will readily accept pinkie mice along with the more traditional invertebrate fare.

In captivity, the Namibian sand gecko is not an overly active species. A pair or a trio may be maintained in a 20-gallon (75.7 L) "long" terrarium, with floor space of 12 × 30 inches (30.5–76.2 cm). Either a desert or a dry savanna setup will suffice. Daytime temperatures of 88 to 92°F (31.1–33.3°C) should be provided for most of the year. Nighttime temperatures can be lowered by several degrees. A slight winter cooling (for about two months, this coinciding with the shortest natural photoperiod) seems to heighten breeding success when temperatures are again raised.

After they have been acclimated, considerable breeding success has been had with wild-caught *Chondrodactylus*. Less success has been had with succeeding generations. Whether this is a dietary or other problem has not yet been ascertained.

The Namibian sand gecko was virtually unknown in American herpetoculture prior to the late 1970s. It then was commonly imported for a few years, only to become rare again in the late 1980s. A few specimens continue to be imported, but prices remain artificially inflated because of the lack of regular breeding success.

The rear head margin of the helmeted gecko, Geckonia chazaliae, *bears enlarged conical scales.*

Currently it is more regularly seen in European than in American herpeto-culture.

The Ocelot Gecko

The ocelot gecko (*Paroedura pictus*) is a small denizen of arid-land and rocky savanna habitats of western,

southern, and eastern Madagascar. An adult size of 5 inches (12.7 cm) is attained. Males may be slightly the larger of the two sexes. Adults are largely terrestrial, but hatchlings and juveniles climb rather agilely.

The ocelot gecko is a nocturnal species that is active during all but the very coldest times of the the year.

Male ocelot geckos are capable of producing "clicks" and "squeaks." They are vocal during the breeding season, at which times territoriality and sexual dominance is at its peak. Because of the tropical latitudes in which the ocelot gecko is found, breeding activity may actually occur over much of the year.

The ocelot gecko occurs in two distinct color and pattern phases. The first is banded with creamish gray against a ground color of deep brown (with advancing age the bands weaken and diffuse into numerous spots). The second phase lacks all but vestiges of bands, bearing instead a prominent light middorsal stripe. Hatchlings and juveniles are some-what more brilliantly colored and pre-

Namib sand geckos are sexually dimorphic. Note the ocelli on the body of the male (rear).

cisely patterned than the adults. Both dorsal and lateral surfaces bear prominently tuberculate scales. The head is large, the body slender. The developing eggs can be seen as diffuse light areas through the lateral and ventral body walls of the female. Each toe is tipped with two leaflike pads.

Despite being agile and fast, this attractive little gecko is not overly active; a pair or trio may be maintained and bred in a 10-gallon (37.9 L) capacity terrarium. A 2-inch (5.1 cm) bottom substrate of peat and sand mixture will allow the females to nest naturally. If the terrarium is misted regularly, the slight moisture buildup in the substrate will provide a suitable incubation medium for the eggs. At a temperature of between 83 and 86°F (28.3–30°C), the incubation time will be a day or two on either side of two months. If you prefer not to have a substrate such as described here, you can use an indoor/outdoor carpet and provide a shallow 4 × 4 inch (10.2 cm^2) plastic dish with 1 inch (2.5 cm) of barely moistened laying medium. The female will seek this out for deposition of her eggs. Pieces of cork bark or other such areas of seclusion must be provided.

Ocelot geckos are both attractive and hardy. Although some are bred by hobbyists, most offered in the pet marketplace are imported specimens. Ocelot geckos feed readily on half-grown crickets, waxworms, and other similarly sized insect fare. They will drink water from a flat dish. Food insects should be dusted with a vitamin D_3 and calcium supplement at least once weekly. These are a tropical species that prefers daytime temperatures of 82 to 88°F (27.8–31.1°C). A drop of several degrees at night is perfectly acceptable. Breeding is probably stimulated by a slight lengthening in the photoperiod as well as by increasing humidity. Because this is a Southern Hemisphere species, ocelot geckos may take a season or

Hatchling Madagascar ocelot geckos, Paroedura pictus, *are much more brilliantly marked than the adults.*

two to acclimate to the reversed seasons of the Northern Hemisphere. These pretty and interesting geckos are deserving of consideration by any hobbyist. They are easy enough to keep and breed to be considered a beginner's species. Ocelot geckos tolerate handling rather well.

Eggs are visible through the thin body walls of many gecko species. Note the egg (mid-body light spot) on this female ocelot gecko.

Day Geckos: The Genus *Phelsuma*

The genus *Phelsuma* contains approximately 60 species of geckos that, because of their propensities for daytime (as well as nighttime) activities, are usually referred to as "day geckos." For the most part restricted to Madagascar and surrounding islands, representatives of the genus also occur in the Seychelles, in the Comoros, on the islands of Réunion and Mauritius, and on Round Island. A single species occurs on the Andaman Islands in India's Bay of Bengal. Two large species, both now extinct, once occurred on the island of Rodriguez. The name "day gecko," although not entirely descriptive, does acknowledge that these (for the most part) wonderfully attractive geckos are active during the daylight hours when most other gecko species are quietly resting. However, the common name fails to call attention to the fact that day geckos are also active well into the hours of darkness.

The day geckos range in size from small (3 inches [7.6 cm]) to large (12 inches [30.5 cm]) with most being somewhere between these two sizes. All have expanded digital disks and lidless eyes bearing round pupils, and most have a green (or at least greenish) ground color (a very few are brown or gray). Day geckos are omnivorous, consuming not only insects but pollen, nectar, overripe fruits, and saps and juices as well. Of the (about) 60 extant species of *Phelsuma*, several are critically imperiled because of continuing habitat degradation.

Although they were once considered difficult captives, in recent years more thorough understanding of their needs has proven many species of day geckos hardy and long-lived.

Important: Day geckos are extremely territorial. Unless your caging facilities are of the "walk-in" or enclosed atrium size, you should not attempt to keep more than a single male and two or three females per terrarium. It is best if all geckos housed in a single enclosure are of a similar size and are introduced to their new quarters simultaneously. Even then, a hierarchy will quickly be established.

Small Species

Spotted Day Gecko

Although the spotted day gecko (*P. guttata*) occasionally attains a length of nearly 5 inches (12.7 cm), most specimens are somewhat less than 4 inches (10.2 cm) in overall length. Neither is *guttata* a particularly heavy-bodied form. Thus, the initial impression is of a small bluish green or light green lizard copiously and variably spotted dorsally and laterally with both brick-red and dark spots. A dark line extends from the snout through the eye and terminates above the tympanum (external eardrum), and the top of the head is patterned with stripes rather than spots.

These are non-egg-gluers, thus the eggs may be easily moved to an incubator.

Fly-sized crickets, small waxworms, and the day gecko formula are all readily consumed.

The spotted day gecko is a species of the scrub and banana trees introduced in an area of eastern Madagascar now stripped of its primary forests. *Guttata* is a hardy species that is, at this time at least, both readily available and relatively inexpensive.

Yellow-headed (neon) Day Gecko

P. klemmeri is a newly discovered form of remarkable beauty. The "yellow" of the head is actually a chartreuse or a lime green. The dorsum is turquoise anteriorly and olive-tan posteriorly. The tail is turquoise, brightest distally. The limbs are olive tan, obscurely peppered with lighter pigment. A broad black lateral line is present from tympanum to groin. This is bordered beneath by the white of the venter. The surface of the head is peppered with tiny black speckles; two blue dots, one in the black post-tympanal stripe and one immediately anterior to the shoulder, are present. This tiny, flattened day gecko attains a 3-inch (7.6 cm) overall length.

Klemmeri is found in coastal northwestern Madagascar, where it dwells on large, rough-barked trees, retreating into bark crevices and hollows when threatened. The flattened conformation stands this species in good stead for such retreat, and dictates that *klemmeri* be maintained in absolutely escape-proof terrariums. These little lizards are able to sidle into and escape through the slightest apertures.

Although this species is not considered an egg-gluer, females that I have maintained have placed their eggs high in leaf sheaths of bamboo as well as inside the hollows of bamboo stems. They will adhere to such surfaces but are easily dislodged.

Fly-sized crickets, termites, springtails, flightless fruit flies, and day gecko formula are all readily consumed.

Yellow-headed day geckos are hardy and easily bred—but caution! If you think the adults are escape artists, just wait until a 1-inch (2.5 cm) long hatchling demonstrates its prowess at escape.

In 1993, the yellow-headed day gecko was being imported in only small numbers. This, and the fact that it is so beautiful, rather assures that the asking price will remain high in the foreseeable future.

Lined Day Gecko

P. lineata ssp. another rather flattened species that, although recorded up to nearly 5 inches (12.7 cm) in length, is more often seen at a length of slightly less than 4 inches (10.2 cm). There are at least five subspecies that, collectively, range over much of the northern half of the island of Madagascar. Habitats range from savanna to rain forests. This appears to be an adaptable species, which colonizes shrubs and remaining trees as the geckos' natural habitat is destroyed. It will be interesting to see whether such adaptation will survive the test of time or if the populations will dwindle and disappear with the passing years. At this moment, at least, the various *lineata* remain rather consistently available and comparatively inexpensive.

The lined day gecko is somewhat dimorphic, the male being a more intense green and larger than the female. Depending on the subspecies, the dorsum may be decorated with numerous isolated red markings or the markings may coalesce into a sizable orange blotch. The orange dorsal blotches or spots are often more prominent posteriorly. The reddish

Profuse orange spots give the spotted day gecko, Phelsuma guttatus, *both common and scientific names.*

The tiny neon day gecko, Phelsuma klemmeri, *is one of the most beautiful species in a brilliantly colored genus.*

Bottom left. According to subspecies and mood, lined day geckos, Phelsuma lineata *ssp., may be either green or brown. Bottom right. The drab day gecko,* Phelsuma mutabilis, *is aptly named.*

lateral stripe (from which the species derives its name) is often bordered with maroon, then white, ventrally.

Captive lined day geckos like to place their eggs in cavities. The hollow ends of suitably sized vertical bamboo shoots are particularly favored. The eggs adhere to their support but with care may be dislodged and moved to the incubator. Although hardy, lined day geckos are not one of the more easily bred species. Additional research is required to better the record with this species.

Although occasionally seen lapping their gecko formula, the few lined day geckos that I have kept have seemed to prefer insects.

Drab Day Gecko

Unlike the majority of its congeners, the drab day gecko (*P. mutabilis*) is clad in scales of variable gray that are overlain dorsally with equally variable lichenate markings. It is indigenous to hot, semiarid western Madagascar. Because of its drab coloration, this is a species that is in demand only by advanced hobbyists. Neophyte day gecko enthusiasts would much prefer to center their interests on more brilliantly colored species. This small, to 4 inches (10.2 cm), western Madagascan species is able to temporarily withstand temperatures in excess of 100°F (37.8°C). The drab day gecko may be found in terrestrial

As a captive, the beautiful blue-tailed day gecko, Phelsuma cepediana, *is one of the more demanding forms.*

The yellow-throated day gecko, Phelsuma flavigularis, *is aptly named.*

Many geckos have no common names. The pretty Phelsuma (laticauda) angularis *from Madagascar is one such.*

The peacock day gecko, Phelsuma quadriocellata, *takes its name from the blue edged dark ocelli usually present on the sides of the body.*

The newly discovered Phelsuma seippi *is a medium sized species commonly known as Seipp's day gecko.*

The horizontally flattened tail and yellow throat of the flat-tailed day gecko, Phelsuma serraticauda, *are diagnostic.*

locations more commonly than most other day gecko species. *P. mutabilis* seems rather easily bred and apparently prefers insect prey over the gecko formula. It is an egg-gluer.

Medium-sized Species

Blue-tailed Day Gecko

The blue-tailed day gecko (*P. cepediana*) is a magnificently colored but rather delicate species. It is sexually dimorphic, the males being the more brilliant and larger of the sexes. There is also considerable variation in pattern and marking intensity, the highlands form being less brilliant than the lowland.

The males are colored an intense turquoise to almost robin's-egg blue dorsally, often patterned with brilliant orange lateral and dorsolateral striping as well as dorsal spots and stripes. The sides of the face and anterior lateral surfaces are intense green. The tail is brilliant blue. Females are usually a rather brilliant green, and although having the markings of the males, these are paler, hence not as well defined. Females of the highland color variant often lack both the lateral and dorsolateral striping and are more heavily spotted dorsally. Although adult males occasionally near a 6-inch (15.2 cm) overall length, 4.5 to 5 inches (11.4–12.7 cm) is the more typical size.

Indigenous to Mauritius, through introduction *cepediana* now also occurs along the east coast of Madagascar.

In the wild, *P. cepediana* is restricted to high-humidity habitats. It also requires high humidity in captivity. It is a species best kept in large cages with myriad live plants. It benefits from frequent and copious mistings. Those that I have kept have done best in the wood and wire walk-in cages described in the caging sec-tion (see page 21). They also best thrived when kept outdoors for the majority of the year, a not unmanageable requirement in southwest Florida. They were especially active and brilliantly colored during our lengthy rainy season.

Both insects and formula are avidly accepted.

This is an egg-gluing species, but breeding successes seem rather limited. Additional research is necessary to fill in gaps in present knowledge.

Yellow-throated Day Gecko

P. flavigularis is 5 inches (12.7 cm) of beautiful green, blue, orange, and yellow. Restricted to the northeastern and northcentral coast of Madagascar, the yellow-throated day gecko seems nowhere common. It is one of the species now under consideration by the Malagasy government for complete protection. In 1993, yellow-throats continued to be exported in small numbers. In spite of this limited availability, they are not one of the truly expensive species.

Although *P. flavigularis* is primarily green dorsally, orange interstices (the skin between the scales) and orange spots are often very visible. This species has blue surrounding the eyes, orange bars bridging the nose, and a lemon yellow throat. The tail is flattened but lacks the serrate edges that typify the otherwise similar flat-tailed day gecko (*P. serraticauda*).

Although the paired eggs of the yellow-throated day geckos are adhesive when first laid, I have found them rather easily dislodged, especially when deposited on the rather yielding leaf of a plant.

This is an aggressive species. The males may so dominate the females that they will have to be removed to a separate terrarium except for the purpose of breeding. This is more often true in a small-sized terrarium than in one of the big, heavily vegetated wood and wire walk-in cages.

The yellow-throat is a hardy species that eagerly accepts both insect prey and day gecko formula.

Gold-dust Day Gecko

Although the specific scientific name, *P. laticauda*, refers to a "flat-tail," this common name is more generally applied to the somewhat larger *P. serraticauda,* a species with not only a flattened but a flanged tail as well. The more accepted common name of gold-dust day gecko refers to the liberal peppering of yellow on the nape and shoulder area of *P. laticauda.* The gold-dust day gecko is usually a brilliant green species that often displays a bluish tinge ventro-laterally and on the limbs and feet. Some specimens may display a yellowish wash on their dorsal surface. A trio of elongated, orange teardrop markings adorn the mid-dorsum. These are followed posteriorly by a varying number of smaller orange markings that may be discrete or coalesce into a vaguely reticulate pattern. This is a 5-inch (12.7 cm) long species.

A smaller, somewhat less colorful subspecies, with an even more flattened tail, exists in northwestern Madagascar. The specific identification of this form is *P. l. angularis.* Some authorities consider it a full species. Besides the other dorsal markings, an inverted orange chevron is present anterior to the teardrops.

The gold-dust day gecko is widely distributed. It not only occurs on Madagascar, but on the Comoro Islands as well, and has been introduced into the Seychelles and three of the Hawaiian Islands.

P. laticauda is a hardy and easily bred species. The eggs are easily incubated, and the hatchlings about 1.5 inches (3.8 cm) in overall length.

Laticauda readily consumes both insect prey and gecko formula.

Peacock Day Gecko

In my estimation *P. quadriocellata* is one of the most beautiful of the day geckos. The specific name of "quadri-ocellata" translates literally to "four spots." The three subspecies are found along much of the eastern coast of Madagascar. The leaf-green dorsum is peppered anteriorly with turquoise. A blue chevron often appears on the snout, its apex above the nostrils. The dorsum is variably marked with orange dots and dashes from the shoulders to the anterior tail. A pair of turquoise-outlined black spots are present posterior to the fore-limbs. A dark marking (usually not actually a spot) is present immediately anterior to each hind limb.

This is basically an arboreal species that commonly attains a rather robust 4.5-inch (11.4 cm) over-all length. Another aggressive species, it may be necessary to separate males from females except for breeding interludes.

The eggs of the peacock day gecko are moderately adhesive when freshly laid. Those laid in the hollows of cut bamboo are usually rather well secured; those affixed to yielding leaves are more easily dislodged. The hatchlings are just a little over 1 inch (2.5 cm) in length when emerging from the paired eggs. Although preferring high humidity, peacock day geckos are hardy and can be prolific breeders if properly cycled.

Seipp's Day Gecko

Although only recently described, the 5.5-inch (13.9 cm) long Seipp's day gecko (*P. seippi*) has already been bred many times in captivity. It is a pretty species with an orange-peppered dorsum of pale green, a well-defined bridle of orange between the eyes, and a prominent maroon chevron extending from the snout to a point well posterior to each eye.

Those that I have maintained were quite tolerant of one another and showed little aggressive behavior. The females placed their paired eggs in terrestrial situations, often beneath pieces of cork bark. The eggs were easily incubated, and the hatchlings were about 1.5-inches (3.8 cm) in overall length.

Seippi occurs in humid areas of northern Madagascar. It seems to prefer a rather high relative humidity in its terrarium.

Flat-tailed Day Gecko

P. serraticauda is another of my favorites. Males of the brilliant green (some are yellowish green) flat-tailed day gecko can near a 6-inch (15.2 cm) overall length. Males also have a proportionately broader tail than the females. The females are 1 inch (2.5 cm) or so smaller. Three maroon bands cross the head, one on the snout, one anterior to the eyes, and the third just posterior to the eyes. The dorsum is often liberally peppered with small orange spots anteriorly and has an orange stripe of variable length on each side of the slightly darker vertebral stripe. Three elongated orange teardrops are present posteriorly. The throat is lemon yellow. Males can be persistently aggressive toward a female, especially if kept paired in a small terrarium. This is less apt to be so if the animals are in a large, heavily

vegetated wood and wire walk-in cage, and even less so if several females are kept to each male. However, the females will interact between themselves in a semi-aggressive manner, quickly establishing a hierarchy.

Healthy, content flat-tailed day geckos breed rather readily in captivity, females producing three or four sets of two eggs each annually. The eggs are quite adhesive when freshly laid and will readily adhere to wood uprights, vertical sections of bamboo, or, more rarely, plant leaves.

Large Species

Giant Day Gecko

In one or another of its four subspecies, the large, attractive *P. madagascariensis* is the hands-down favorite among hobbyists. It is the only one of the day geckos that the dealers routinely designate by subspecies. All of the four subspecies have been bred extensively in captivity, with most emphasis seemingly placed on the subspecies *grandis* and *madagascariensis*. Courtship is aggressive, and many visual barriers and plenty of space are necessary to prevent the females being injured by the larger males. The giant day gecko is highly arboreal, and as such does best in heavily planted, vertically oriented terrariums or the large wood and wire walk-in cages described earlier (see page 21).

Egg-laying females orient themselves nearly vertically between the leaves of stiff-leafed plants such as sansevierias, bananas, or, in captivity, bromeliads. They lay an egg, hold it in the rear feet until the shell has dried, place the egg deep in the axils of the plant in which they are positioned, then repeat the process with the second of the two-egg clutch. The eggs are nonadhesive and can be easily removed to an incubator.

This is (arguably) the largest of Madagascar's day geckos, the largest examples of the largest subspecies attaining 1 foot (30.5 cm) in length.

All subspecies will eagerly accept suitably sized insect prey and avidly consume their gecko formula.

The subspecies of the giant day gecko are:

Boehm's Giant Day Gecko

P. m. boehmi is restricted in distribution to the central eastern coast of Madagascar. The largest markings are in the forms of dots and dashes on the dorsal surface of the head. A broad ocular stripe is present, beginning above the tympanum and converging on the tip of the snout. Numerous orange dots and short dashes are present over most of the dorsum. The lateral scales are prominent and noticeably tuberculate. Adults are somewhat less than 9 inches (22.9 cm) in length. This is not a commonly offered race of giant day gecko.

Madagascar Giant Day Gecko

P. m. grandis adults regularly exceed a 10-inch (25.4 cm) length and seem to top out at about 1 foot (30.5 cm). Males attain a larger size than the females. This is a bright green subspecies with prominent maroon head markings and equally prominent (usually), well-defined orange dorsal markings. Occasionally some blue is present, especially on the sides of the head. The amount of orange present seems to vary individually, and cannot be used as a characteristic to determine geographic origin of the lizard. These are remarkably impressive geckos. This remains an abundant race that is widely spread in northern Madagascar and on the surrounding islands.

Koch's Giant Day Gecko

Most unicolored of the group, *P. m. kochi* has granular scales that are prominently tuberculate on the sides and jowls. All of the orange highlights, so prominent on the remaining three races, are greatly reduced in intensity. This race occurs in western and northwestern Madagascar. It is highly arboreal, but often suns while positioning itself head downward on the trunk of a tree. Although usually about 9 inches (22.9 cm) in overall length, this race can attain an imposing 12 inches (30.5 cm).

Madagascar Day Gecko

P. m. madagascariensis is smaller than *grandis* (note that the word "giant" is omitted from the common name of this 9-inch (22.9 cm) long race). It ranges widely in eastern Madagascar as well as some of the eastern islands. A population also exists near the southeastern city of Taolonaro. A maroon ocular stripe is usually present. The orange spots on the dorsal surface of the head are usually only weakly defined. The green of the dorsum can be variable, ranging from light to dark green. The orange spots of the dorsum are often arranged in three weakly defined longitudinal rows, the vertebral row being the best defined. The lateral scales are tuberculate, those of the jowls prominently so.

Standing's Day Gecko

P. standingi is the second of the two contenders for Madagascar's largest day gecko species. Standing's day gecko, large and grayish green or bluish green when adult, is prominently banded with russet and blue-gray when hatched. Adult males attain 1 foot (30.5 cm) in length. Females are marginally smaller. This is a heavy-bodied, very impressive species. Although lacking the brilliance of the earlier species, Standing's day geckos display a subtle beauty in their coloration.

Until recently, Standing's day geckos have been infrequently seen in the pet trade. Now that this species from arid southwestern Madagascar is seen more regularly in the pet trade, concern is being voiced about its well-being in the wild. It seems that not only are the animals being collected now, but their habitat is being eradicated by the charcoal trade as well.

When properly cared for, Standing's day geckos are long-lived. I have a trio, already large adults when received, that have now exceeded a decade in captivity. They show no signs of slowing down yet, continuing to breed regularly and showing every other sign of continuing vitality, as well. Now kept in a large walk-in cage on the side deck, these lizards have time and again experienced nighttime temperatures in the high 30s and low 40sF (0–7°C) with no signs of distress. They quickly access their basking perches with the rising of the sun and are soon foraging for crickets, giant mealworms, and the gecko formula. Although this trio of Standing's geckos are quite compatible, new adult specimens are quickly set upon by both the male and the two females; this even in the large, well planted walk-in cage in which they now reside. Little or no attention is given by the adults to juveniles, but when sexual maturity is reached they are mercilessly badgered, necessitating removal.

Captive Care and Breeding

Stress

Day geckos kept too cool, too crowded, or too hot, or subjected to aggression by dominant terrarium mates will display certain signs of stress. Among these are a tendency for the subordinate specimen(s) to continually hide, to lack a feeding response, to be continually fearful and nervous, and to persistently display an abnormal coloration (usually dark). Stress can prove fatal to an otherwise healthy gecko. Observe your day geckos frequently and get to know what are, for yours, normal colors and responses. Certain species are more aggressive toward tankmates than others. Stress may be reduced by adding visual barriers, by placing your animals in a larger cage, by adjusting cage temperature, or by adding additional females. If, after all of these corrective measures stress continues, you will have no choice but to separate your specimens into individual terrariums. If this becomes necessary, it is usually possible to periodically move the male to the female's container for the purpose of breeding. Watch carefully for signs of overt aggressiveness toward the female by the male. It may be necessary to again separate the two almost immediately. If relatively compatible, it still may be necessary to again separate the two after breeding has been accomplished. Observe and be ready to take whatever steps are necessary.

Housing

Because of their remarkable brilliance and small size, most day geckos are ideal candidates for inclusion in the tropical woodland terrarium. The size of the terrariums should be dictated by the adult size of the day geckos retained therein. Because they are persistently arboreal, day geckos do best in a "tall" terrarium. Day geckos do not tolerate crowding well. For a pair or trio of small to moderately sized geckos, a 15-gallon (56.8 L) tall tank will provide sufficient space. For a pair or trio of the large species, I suggest nothing smaller than a 30-gallon (113.6 L) tall terrarium, and prefer a 50- to 80-gallon (189.3–302.8 L) size. If constrained too tightly, day geckos may survive but won't thrive. A trio of Standing's day geckos that I have had

for more than ten years now thrived and bred for five of those years in a 65-gallon (246.1 L) hexagonal terrarium in the corner of the living room. The tank was well lit, having both a fluorescent fixture fitted with a Vita-Lite bulb and an incandescent "plant-grow" floodlight. This latter provided warmth as well as illumination. A large hollow log, a few cross branches of bamboo, and a wildly clambering *Epipremnum aureus* ("pothos" or variegated philodendron) provided security, visual barriers, a feeding platform, and multiple drinking stations. To provide drinking water for the lizards, the leaves of the plant were misted daily with tepid water. The substrate was merely 4 inches (10.2 cm) of sterilized potting soil. Eggs were laid on the substrate inside the almost upright hollow log. From there, the eggs were easily gathered and incubated.

An Ideal *Phelsuma* Caging Facility

I believe in providing as much room as possible for any captive reptiles with which I work. I have found that a wire-covered wood-frame cage of almost walk-in size is ideal for the day geckos and, because of its easy cleaning features, great for me.

The top and bottom of the cage are made of 0.75 inch (19.1 mm) exterior plywood. The center of the top has been removed, leaving only a 6-inch (15.2 cm) wide rim all around. I have found this approach gives greater stability than a top framed in with 2×2 inch (5.1×5.1 cm) lumber. The uprights and door are made from carefully chosen *straight* pressure-treated 2×2 inch (5.1×5.1 cm) lumber. The wire is 0.125 inch (3.2 mm) mesh hardware cloth (this size will retain all but the smallest crickets). The whole cage is mounted on large casters to facilitate easy moving.

Suggested dimensions: 6 feet (1.8 m) high (including casters) by 4 feet

A "tall" terrarium with hiding area, multiple drinking areas and basking areas will house a trio of Phelsuma.

Two Easily Made and Stored Artificial Diets for Your Day Geckos

Michael Miller, D.V.M., was one of the pioneers in day gecko diet research. His tried and true formula consisted of:

2 bottles of strained mixed fruit baby food
5 eyedroppersful of Avitron liquid bird vitamins
1 teaspoon of bee pollen (available at health food stores)
10 ccs of 20 percent calcium gluconate
1 teaspoon liquid form vitamin C
Add water to a soupy consistency—about 4 parts ingredients and 5 parts water.

Of course Miller was feeding a room full of breeding Phelsuma at the time. To feed one or two pairs, you could use this formula but proportionately reduce the quantities of all ingredients.

The formula I have used successfully over the years is simpler yet:
⅓ jar of mixed fruit or apricot strained baby food
⅓ jar of strained papaya baby food
1 teaspoon of honey
⅓ eyedropper of Avitron liquid bird vitamins
½ teaspoon of Osteoform powdered vitamins
Add water to a proper soupy consistency.

Occasionally when I have bee pollen available, I add a small amount. The geckos do not seem to care, either way.

Refrigerate both formulas between uses. Check to make sure this does not sour or ferment in the refrigerator.

The hatchlings of Seipp's day gecko are less colorful than the adults.

(1.2 m) long, just narrow enough to fit through interior doors. The dimensions of the hinged door are 24 (width) × 48 (height) inches (61 × 122 cm). The wire is fastened to the frame using stainless staples 0.75 inch (19.1 mm) long from a standard staple gun. Those that don't seat tightly are tapped in with a hammer. A potted ficus tree is placed within, and several sizable branches provide additional perches. Vining philodendron clambers across the bottom. For cleaning, the cage is rolled outside and hosed down thoroughly. The cage remains out on a sunny deck from mid-spring to late autumn. It is brought out on suitable days all year long. During the winter, 4-mil plastic sheeting is stapled over the wire on three sides and the top to lessen the cool breezes and concentrate the heat from the winter sun.

Some Terrarium Basics: Both horizontal and vertical perches are necessary to the well-being of day geckos. Illuminate and warm at least one of the horizontal perches (preferably two) to provide a suitable basking area for your geckos. Sections of bamboo are ideal perch material. Tank-length sections can be held in place by a dollop of latex aquarium sealant on each end. If you are keeping more than a single day gecko per terrarium, visual barriers are desired and may even be imperative to prevent intraspecific aggression. The adage "out of sight, out of mind" aptly applies here. The visual barriers can be provided by utilizing a crisscross of bamboo lengths, a suitably sized vining plant, or a combination of the two. Day geckos prefer to drink by lapping pendulous droplets of water from freshly misted plant leaves or bamboo sections. Many day geckos will steadfastly refuse to drink from a water dish. Mist the leaves of your plants with tepid water daily. Be certain that the plants you use have not been freshly sprayed with insecticides or liquid fertilizers. Grow commercially procured plants for a couple of weeks outside of the terrarium to allow systemic additives a chance to dissipate. To grow in a terrarium, plants (even forest plants) will need strong lighting. Incandescent fixtures using a commercial plant-grow floodlight bulb are ideal. These bulbs will provide warmth for your geckos as well as the necessary illumination for the plants. In addition, a fluorescent full-spectrum bulb should be used. This will provide small amounts of ultraviolet (UV-A and UV-B) rays for your geckos. These UV rays assist reptiles in properly metabolizing vitamins and minerals and in promoting natural behavior by the lizards.

Nutrition

As mentioned earlier, day geckos have complex (but, fortunately, rather easily duplicated) diets. They not only consume insects, but seek out nectars, pollens, exudates from overripe fruits and the fruits themselves, and plant saps as well.

The fondness of day geckos for sweet fruit and flower byproducts offers you a simple way of administering the necessary vitamin and mineral supplements, as well. Without these latter, especially vitamin D_3 and calcium, day geckos are quite apt to develop a metabolic bone disorder (once simply called "decalcification" or "rubber bone disease"). Rapidly growing young and female geckos that are utilizing calcium to form shells for their developing eggs will be affected more quickly than adult males or nonovulating females. Ideally, the ratio of calcium to phosphorus should be two to one and of vitamin D_3 to vitamin A, one to one. A lack of vitamin D_3 (which enhances calcium metabolism) or an excess of vitamin A can cause skeletal demineralization and deformities. The use of vitamin and mineral supplements is necessary even with full-spectrum lighting.

Either of the formulas (see page 96) is suitable for virtually all species of day geckos. I have kept and bred more than a half-dozen species over the years. These have ranged from the tiny yellow-headed day gecko (*P. klemmeri*) to the large and robust Standing's day gecko (*P. standingi*).

Besides the vitamin-enhanced fruit mixture, I provide the geckos with calcium-dusted crickets, waxworms, and an occasional giant mealworm. The size of the insects necessarily varies with the size of the geckos being fed. The 3-inch (7.6 cm) long yellow-heads require fly-sized crickets; the 1 foot (30.5 cm) long Standing's day geckos relish larger insects.

Reproduction

One of the greatest thrills and challenges for those of us who maintain reptiles is to successfully breed them. Fortunately, most day geckos respond well to captive conditions. If certain minimum criteria are met or exceeded, many species are rather easily bred. Depending on the species, day geckos may deposit their clutches in one of two ways: they may be either "egg-gluers" or "non-gluers."

Egg-gluers: These eggs are often the more difficult to deal with. If the female gecko chooses a side panel or corner of her terrarium on which to glue the eggs, the whole enclosure will need to be kept at the suggested incubation temperature of from 78 to 86°F (25.6–30°C). If the female gecko deposits her eggs on a removable item (flowerpot or plant leaf), then that item can be removed and kept at a proper temperature.

Besides suitable temperature, a high humidity is necessary to successfully incubate gecko eggs (see page 44).

Non-gluers: The eggs of the non-gluers may be removed from their deposition site to where they are to be incubated. Again, a temperature of from 78 to 86°F (25.6–30°C) and a high humidity are desired.

Incubation media: Either fine vermiculite or sphagnum moss, moistened to a proper consistency and kept at a suitable temperature, is an excellent incubation medium. (See page 44)

Incubation duration: Depending on the species of your geckos and the temperature at which the eggs are incubated, the incubation interval will usually be between six and twelve weeks.

Incubation temperature: Temperature will determine both the duration of incubation and the sex of your hatchlings. Varying temperatures, from 77 to 85°F (25–29.4°C), will usually produce geckos of both sexes. Eggs incubated at the warmer end of the temperature range usually produce males, those at the cooler end, females (see chart, page 64).

My tip: A reminder about vitamins, minerals, lighting, and territoriality: It is *mandatory* that captive day geckos be provided with vitamin and mineral supplements. Vitamin D_3 and calcium are the two most important additives. During inclement weather or in indoor facilities, full-spectrum lighting is also necessary. Day geckos—especially the males—are extremely territorial. Although most hobbyists raise many juveniles in the same enclosure, as all reach sexual maturity, males will develop aggressive behavior. Subordinate males will need to be removed to their own individual terrariums. Although day geckos do well in pairs, I have found two or three females to a single male seems a better ratio. Such groupings are more visible and seem to thrive better. Also, there is, undeniably, a potential for more fertilized eggs.

Handling Your Day Gecko

The easiest and most concise instruction I can offer regarding handling day geckos is the single word, "*don't.*" Don't handle them!

Beautiful though those skins may be, they are remarkably easy to tear. Additionally, a mere bump may cause the tail to autotomize.

Day geckos are alert and fast. They become even more so at the slightest hint of danger. To even long-term captives, an approaching hand equates to grave danger.

If it does become necessary to handle your day geckos, do so firmly but gently. Allowing them to squirm in your grasp will only accentuate the possibility of their skin being torn. Most tears will heal over quickly, and even considerable scars will virtually disappear after several sheds.

Photographing Geckos

Photographing reptiles can be a demanding but fulfilling pursuit. Many hobbyists see photography as the best way to document captive or wild behavior patterns. Good slides are certainly excellent educational tools. Photography is a pursuit that I enjoy immensely. Capturing a gecko—even a relatively inactive gecko—on film often requires a great deal of patience and discipline. Each photo helps you to see how the next could be improved. Getting started in photography is easy but can be expensive.

The equipment required will depend upon a number of variables. Among these are whether you will be indulging in both long-distance field photos and staged close-ups. Of course, photographing captive or staged lizards is infinitely easier than pursuing and photographing free-ranging ones, but some feel it not nearly as satisfying.

Basic Equipment

A sturdy 35-mm camera body with interchangeable lenses is suggested. You don't necessarily need a brand-new camera body and lenses; I've used quality secondhand equipment for many of my photographic ventures. You do need a photo supply dealer who can advise you about the condition of the equipment you're buying, and who can tell you about some features of that particular lens or body (usually speaking, secondhand camera equipment does not come with manuals of any sort).

Lenses: The lenses I use include: 28-mm wide angle for habitat photos; 50-mm standard for habitat photos; 100-mm macro for close-ups (suitable for almost every purpose); 75–205-mm zoom lens for variable fieldwork; 400-mm fixed focal length telephoto lens for fieldwork; 120–600-mm zoom lens for distant but variable fieldwork.

Strobes: A series of dedicated strobes (a dedicated strobe interfaces with the camera f-stop setting to furnish appropriate light levels).

Lens adapter: An ×1.25 power magnifyer or an ×2 doubler.

Film: ISO 50 slide film is slower and less "grainy" than higher-speed films. This slower film will give you the best results, but also requires a bright day or electronic flashes to compensate for the slow speed. The higher the ISO of the film, the less light you will need to photograph, but the "grainier" your pictures will be. If you are taking pictures with the hopes of having them published, use ISO 50 slide film and adapt your methods to its requirements. If you are taking photos merely for your own enjoyment, use either slide or print film, as you prefer.

Tripod: A sturdy tripod (an absolute necessity for the telephoto lenses) will hold your camera steady while you squeeze off that "once in a lifetime" shot. Camera equipment with lenses is heavy, especially if you're out in the field and have slogged through hip-deep water, then scaled a couple of hillsides. The equipment is heavy even if you're indoors.

Camera body: After having a camera body malfunction on occasion, I now always have at least one spare body available. This is especially important if you are photographing in the field.

Some Photographic Hints

For staged photography, create a small natural setting by placing rocks, mosses, leaves, or bark—whichever is most appropriate for the species you're photographing—on a stage. In the past, I used a small lazy Susan as a stage, thinking I could rotate the stage with the animal on it, for different photographic angles. This works, providing that you move *very slowly*, both in your own actions and in rotating the stage. If you don't have a lazy Susan, just arrange the setting items on a tabletop or on a tree stump (outdoors or in), put the lizard in place, focus, and shoot. Having a photo assistant to help pose or catch the (escaping) gecko (whichever is applicable) will help.

I created a backing for my stage with the top half of a heavy-duty round plastic trash can. I first cut it to size, then firmly bolted it in place. Black velvet clipped into place around the inside surface of the background gives a good background for the lizard shots. The result is an easily moved, emminently serviceable stage.

Field photography can be considerably more trying than staged photography. To successfully accomplish the former, it is almost mandatory that you have an assistant.

Approaching a nocturnal gecko with a camera, all the while keeping the lizard in the beam from a flashlight, can be truly exasperating. Generally, if you move very slowly, the lizard will remain in place long enough to permit you to get a few shots. You, or your partner, will need to move quickly to capture the gecko if it moves. I generally try to first make field photos, then capture this specimen and take staged photos. Between the two approaches, I often get excellent results.

If you're trying field photography, approach the animal slowly and obliquely. Avoid eye contact. If the lizard notices you (and of course it will!) freeze for a moment, then begin moving again. Eventually, if you are lucky, you will be close enough to make the field shot for which you were hoping.

Geckos at Zoos

Fortunately, geckos of many kind thrive as captives. Many species, some of them quite rare in the private sector, can be seen at zoos across the world.

In the United States, the Ft. Worth (Texas) Zoo has a large and varied collection of geckos. Among the common forms, one can see such rarities as reticulated, helmeted, northland green, several of the New Caledonian prehensile-tailed, and various Madagascan leaf-tailed geckos.

The Dallas (Texas) Zoo also has a magnificent collection of common and rare species.

The San Diego (California) Zoo is the only one of the United States zoos to report having the strange little Australian knob-tailed gecko (*Nephrurus levis*).

Chaffee Zoological Gardens in Fresno, California, has many of the more uncommon day geckos, several species of the New Caledonian prehensile-tailed geckos, and the beautiful northland green geckos from New Zealand.

Audubon Zoological Gardens in New Orleans, Louisiana, has reported the only Australian leaf-toed geckos in the United States.

Houston, Texas has barking geckos and many other species.

The Memphis (Tennessee) Zoo maintains yellow-headed and other small gecko species.

Useful Addresses and Literature

Gecko Sources

Geckos that once were rare in the private sector are increasingly available from both private and commercial breeders and importers.

Many sources advertise in the various reptile and amphibian magazines. If I were looking for a particular species, I would check the ads in the following publications:

Reptiles Magazine
P.O. Box 6050
Mission Viejo, California 92690

Reptile and Amphibian Magazine
RD 3, Box 3709-A
Pottsville, Pennsylvania 17901

Reptilian Magazine
22 Firs Close
Hazlemere, High Wycombe
Buck HP15 7HF, England

The Vivarium (the publication of the American Federation of Herpetoculturists)
P.O. Box 300067
Escondido, California 92030

Affinity Groups

Herpetological/herpetocultural clubs can be found in many large cities. Check with the biology department of your nearest university or with the personnel of nature centers or museums to find the location of the club nearest you.

The International Gecko Society
P.O. Box 370423
San Diego, California 92137-0423

This society is an excellent source of information for gecko enthusiasts. It produces the informative, high-quality, quarterly journal *Dactylus*.

Books and Articles

Until quite recently, there was a dearth of published data about geckos. Although this is slowly changing, you will still need to search among the field guides, scientific journals, and the very occasional husbandry article to find information.

Arnold, E. N. and J. A. Burton. *A Field Guide to the Reptiles and Amphibians of Britain and Europe.* London: Collins, 1978.

Bartlett, R. D. "*Phelsuma klemmeri*: The Neon Tetra of Geckos." *Reptiles Magazine.* Vol. 1, no. 2, 1993.

_____ "Notes on Standing's Day Gecko." *Tropical Fish Hobbyist Magazine.* Vol. XLII, no. 1, 1993.

Cogger, Harold A. *Reptiles and Amphibians of Australia.* Ithaca: Cornell, 1992.

Conant, Roger and Joseph T. Collins. *Reptiles and Amphibians, Eastern/Central North America.* Boston: Houghton Mifflin, 1991.

Frye, Fredric L. *A Practical Guide for Feeding Captive Reptiles.* Krieger Publishing Co., Melbourne, Florida, 1991.

Glaw, F. and M. Vences. *A Field Guide to the Amphibians and Reptiles of Madagascar.* Leverkusen: Moos-Druck, 1992.

Halliday, Tim and Kraig Adler. *The Encyclopedia of Reptiles and Amphibians.* New York: Facts on File. 1986.

Jes, Harold. *Lizards in the Terrarium.* Hauppauge, New York: Barron's Educational Series, 1987.

McKeown, Sean. *The General Care and Maintenance of Day Geckos.* Lakeside, California, Advanced Vivarium Systems, 1993.

Peters, James A. *Dictionary of Herpetology.* New York: Hafner, 1964.

_____ and Roberto Donoso-Barros. *Catalogue of Neotropical, Squamata: Part II. Lizards and Amphisbaenians.* Washington: Smithsonian, 1970.

Schwartz, Albert and Robert W. Henderson. *Amphibians and Reptiles of the West Indies.* Gainesville, Florida: University of Florida Press, 1991.

Slavens, Frank and Kate Slavens. *Reptiles and Amphibians in Captivity; Breeding, Longevity and Inventory, Current January 1, 1993.* Seattle: Slaveware, 1993.

Smith, Hobart M. *Handbook of Lizards.* Ithaca: Comstock, 1946.

_____ and Edward H. Taylor. *Herpetology of Mexico,* Ashton, Maryland: Eric Lundberg, 1966.

Stebbins, Robert C. *A Field Guide to Western Reptiles and Amphibians.* Boston: Houghton Mifflin, 1985.

Wareham, David C. *The Reptile and Amphibian Keeper's Dictionary.* London: Blandford, 1993.

Zhao, Er-Mi and Kraig Adler. *Herpetology of China.* Lawrence: SSAR, 1993.

Glossary

Aestivation a period of warm-weather inactivity, often triggered by excessive heat or drought

Allopatric not occurring together but often adjacent

Ambient temperature the temperature of the surrounding environment

Anterior toward the front

Anus the external opening of the cloaca; the vent

Arboreal tree-dwelling

Autotomize the ability to break easily or voluntarily cast off (and usually to regenerate) a part of the body, such as a tail

Brille the clear spectacle that protects the eyes of lidless-eyed geckos

Brumation the reptilian and amphibian equivalent of mammalian hibernation

Caudal pertaining to the tail

Cloaca the common chamber into which digestive, urinary and reproductive systems empty and which itself opens exteriorly through the vent

Con a prefix indicating "the same" (Congeneric refers to species in the same genus).

Crepuscular active at dusk or dawn

Deposition the laying of eggs

Deposition site spot chosen by the female to lay eggs

Dichromatic two color phases of the same species, often sex-linked

Dimorphic a difference of form, build, or coloration in the same species; often sex-linked

Diurnal active in the daytime

Dorsal pertaining to the back; upper surface

Dorsolateral pertaining to the upper sides

Dorsum the upper surface

Endemic Confined to a region

Endolymphatic sacs the sacs of calcium carbonate located on both sides of the neck in certain members of the subfamily Gekkoninae

Femoral pores openings on the underside of the thighs of lizards that produce a waxy exudate

Femur the part of the leg between the hip and the knee

Form an identifiable species or subspecies

Fracture planes softer areas in the tail vertebrae that allow the tail to break easily

Genus a taxonomic classification of a group of species having similar characteristics, falls between the next higher designation of family and the next lower designation of species

Granular pertaining to small, flat scales

Gravid the reptilian equivalent of mammalian pregnancy

Gular pertaining to the throat

Heliothermic pertaining to a species that basks in the sun to thermoregulate

Hemipenes the dual copulatory organs of male lizards and snakes

Hybrid offspring resulting from the breeding of two species

Hydrate to restore body moisture by drinking or absorption

Insular island-dwelling

Intergrade offspring from the breeding of two subspecies

Juvenile young or immature

Keel a ridge (along the center of a scale)

Labial pertaining to the lips

Lamellae the transverse scales that extend across the underside of a gecko's toes

Lateral pertaining to the side

Melanism a profusion of black pigment

Middorsal pertaining to the middle of the back

Midventral pertaining to the center of the abdomen

Monotypic containing but one type

Nocturnal active at night

Oviparous reproducing by means of eggs that hatch after laying

Ovoviviparous reproducing by shelled or membrane-contained eggs that hatch prior to, or at, deposition

Parietal eye a sensory organ present in certain reptiles that is positioned mid-cranially

Phalanges the toe bones

Poikilothermic a species with no internal body temperature regulation; "cold-blooded"

Posterior toward the rear

Preanal pores a series of pores, often in the shape of an anteriorly directed chevron, and located anterior to the anus

Race a subspecies

Rugose not smooth; wrinkled or tuberculate

Saxicolous rock-dwelling

Scansorial capable of or adapted for climbing

Serrate sawlike

Setae the hairlike bristles in the lamellae of a gecko's toes

Spatulae the flattened distal ends of the setae

Species a group of similar creatures that produce viable young when breeding

Subcaudal beneath the tail

Subdigital beneath the toes

Subspecies the subdivision of a species; a race that may differ slightly in color, size, scalation, or other criteria

Sympatric occurring together

Taxonomy science of classification of plants and animals

Terrestrial land-dwelling

Thermoregulate to regulate (body) temperature by choosing a warmer or cooler environment

Thigmothermic pertaining to a species (often nocturnal) that thermoregulates by being in contact with a preheated surface such as a boulder or tarred road surface

Tubercles warty protuberances

Tuberculate pertaining to tubercles

Tympanum the external eardrum

Vent the external opening of the cloaca; the anus

Venter the underside of a creature; the belly

Ventral pertaining to the undersurface or belly

Ventrolateral pertaining to the sides of the venter (belly)

Index

Numerals in **bold face type** indicate color photos. **C1** indicates front cover; **C2**, inside front cover; **C3**, inside back cover; **C4**, back cover.